RAND CORPORATION

T0302952

Making Victory Count After Defeating ISIS

Stabilization Challenges in Mosul and Beyond

Shelly Culbertson, Linda Robinson

For more information on this publication, visit www.rand.org/t/RR2076

Library of Congress Cataloging-in-Publication Data is available for this publication.
ISBN: 978-0-8330-9859-7

Published by the RAND Corporation, Santa Monica, Calif.

Cover image by Mstyslav Chernov.

Preface

The fate of Mosul, Iraq's second-largest city, its largest Sunni-majority city, and the largest city captured by the Islamic State of Iraq and Syria (ISIS), is critical to efforts to permanently defeat the terrorist group and create a stable Iraq. This report focuses on the aftermath of the major combat operations in Mosul, the management of civilian needs (including returning home after displacement), and the requirements for achieving lasting stability in Mosul and other combat-affected areas of Iraq. The authors conducted extensive field research in Iraq at the local and national levels, including case studies of stabilization efforts after battles in major urban centers such as Ramadi, Fallujah, and Tikrit.

The issues identified as related to Mosul also mirror the broader requirements for stability throughout the conflict-affected areas of Iraq. In addition, many of the challenges and solutions identified will require action by the national government and policies that address the underlying issues, whether they pertain to sufficient prioritization and funding of programs, development of adequate professional security forces, or reconciliation measures to resolve conflicts among Iraq's principal political groups. The recommendations and prioritization scheme offered in the final chapter are thus directed at the national government of Iraq and the key stakeholders in the international community.

The report should be helpful to planning efforts by the U.S., Iraqi, and Kurdistan regional governments, as well as the international community, which is playing a significant role through the United Nations, the Global Coalition to Counter ISIS, and bilateral efforts. The report makes a unique contribution by gathering timely primary source materials from key officials in government, military, and aid agencies with leadership responsibilities related to these issues; addressing the crosscutting humanitarian, stabilization, and political challenges; and offering recommendations that are crucial for the stabilization of Mosul and other areas to ensure that the campaign to defeat ISIS is ultimately successful.

RAND Ventures

RAND is a research organization that develops solutions to public policy challenges to help make communities throughout the world safer and more secure, healthier, and more prosperous. RAND is nonprofit, nonpartisan, and committed to the public interest.

RAND Ventures is a vehicle for investing in policy solutions. Philanthropic contributions support our ability to take the long view, tackle tough and often-controversial topics, and share our findings in innovative and compelling ways. RAND's research findings and recommendations are based on data and evidence, and therefore do not necessarily reflect the policy preferences or interests of its clients, donors, or supporters.

Funding for this venture was made possible by the independent research and development provisions of RAND's contracts for the operation of its U.S. Department of Defense federally funded research and development centers.

This research was conducted within the International Security and Defense Policy Center of the RAND National Security Research Division (NSRD). NSRD conducts research and analysis on defense and national security topics for the United States and allied defense, foreign policy, homeland security, and intelligence communities, as well as foundations and other nongovernmental organizations that support defense and national security analys is. For more information on the International Security and Defense Policy Center, see www.rand.org/ndri/centers/isdp or contact the director (con-tact information is provided on the web page).

Contents

Figures, Table, and Boxes

Table

Figures

Boxes

Summary

This report investigates the current status of humanitarian and stabilization efforts in Iraq and particularly Mosul, the capital of Iraq's Ninewa Province. The study is based on exhaustive data collection and review; field visits to Iraq (Erbil, Baghdad, the Khazer displacement camps outside Mosul, and the Qayarah and Hammam al-Alil military bases); and over 50 in-depth interviews with a range of senior officials from the Iraqi government, the United States, other officials from the Global Coalition to Counter ISIS, the United Nations and other multilateral agencies, and implementing nongovernmental organizations. The research team reviewed the humanitarian response plan and the stabilization programs, as well as the track records of implementation through April 2017. Three case studies were conducted on postcombat stabilization efforts in Ramadi, Fallujah, and Tikrit. The researchers recognize that humanitarian and stabilization efforts are intrinsically multifaceted and mutually reinforcing, so we have examined the primary areas of humanitarian activity and pillars of stabilization to include immediate needs, security, infrastructure and services, and governance and reconciliation. All of these activities in turn will affect whether and when civilians are able to return home.

The report focuses on identifying the key gaps in the current effort that will impede further progress and ultimate success. The approach taken by the authors of this report is to identify urgent and primary gaps, which, if filled, will make possible the next steps in recovery. The report does not detail all of the activities needed to enable Iraqis to return to normal lives. In reality, the degree of suffering and destruction throughout recent decades necessitates a long-term commitment by Iraq's government and the international community to repairing the country. The study team's analysis found that the issues that will determine whether Mosul is successfully stabilized mirror, in large part, the issues in the other conflict-affected areas. This is particularly true of the security, governance, and reconciliation issues identified. Moreover, the actions needed are in great part dependent on Iraq's national government plans, decisions, and implementation, as well as support and funding from the international community. Thus, many of the recommendations pertain not only to Mosul but also to the overall stabilization effort in Iraq, and they require full engagement by the national government and its supporters.

The report concludes that without significantly increased effort by Iraqis, the United States and other Coalition officials, and the United Nations, another wave of violence could engulf Iraq in a matter of months if stabilization activities are insufficiently robust. The prospect exists that military victory will dislodge the Islamic State of Iraq and Syria (ISIS), only for Iraq to fall into an extended period of violence and suffering, if the underlying causes of discontent are not addressed and if many of Iraq's 3 million remaining internally displaced persons (IDPs) remain unable to return home. Ongoing instability in Iraq could in turn precipitate further international refugee flows into other Middle Eastern countries and Europe.

The United States, Iraq, and the international community have invested a great deal of effort in removing ISIS from the territories of Iraq and Syria. These efforts and resources will be wasted if they fail to consolidate the gains earned through combat by securing the peace through adequate humanitarian and stabilization measures. The results achieved thus far demonstrate that success is possible through a moderate but thoughtfully applied set of programs that leverage the will and know-how of local and international actors.

The Humanitarian Response

As the battle for Mosul unfolded, by July 2017, a total of over a million people from Mosul had been displaced by the military operations; some 200,000 had returned home. Challenges for providing aid to civilians remaining inside West Mosul during the fighting also increased. In addition, the longer-term displacement of people in 2014 and 2015 by ISIS remained a challenge in terms of both meeting their immediate needs and addressing their eventual return, local integration, or resettlement elsewhere.

The greatest humanitarian issues for people inside Mosul included acute food insecurity, destruction of water supplies, living amid ongoing fighting, security barriers to the provision of aid, and a shortage of urgent health care.

Most IDPs generated by the offensive have moved to displacement camps. The greatest humanitarian challenges facing this group related to protection and health care. IDPs in some of the camps managed by the Kurdistan Regional Government (KRG) were not permitted to leave because of KRG concerns about security. But restricting the movement of IDPs to camps is in direct violation of international norms. Protection concerns also included a lack of uniform screening processes, family separation, and confiscated or missing documentation. In addition, 24-hour physical and mental health care were lacking.

IDPs who fled Mosul and other parts of Ninewa Province because of ISIS in 2014–2015 faced a different set of challenges that included poverty, low education rates, and dwindling assistance because of the longevity of their situation. Many did not want to return to their homes because they feared for their security. The presence of large numbers of IDPs in cities and towns placed enormous strains on their resources. The Kurdistan Region in particular has borne the brunt of these costs in northern Iraq.

Postcombat Security Conditions

Three essential challenges were identified for providing security in Ninewa; these issues also pertain to the other conflict areas of Anbar, Salah al-Din, Kirkuk, and Diyala provinces.

The first urgent challenge is to address the widespread incidence of explosive hazards left by ISIS. Public infrastructure, utilities, and housing were extensively mined and booby-trapped, posing safety risks to those remaining and preventing IDPs from returning home. Explosive hazard mitigation in liberated parts of Iraq enabled some public services to resume, yet these remained vastly insufficient compared to the problem's scope.

The second urgent security need is to provide immediate security through adequate hold forces that would remain in liberated areas after combat operations. The estimated 1.2 million population of Mosul would require a hold force of 60,000 troops, entailing reliance on the Iraqi army, federal police, peshmerga (KRG military forces), and tribal forces. Despite the patchwork of forces and the largely Shia composition of the army and federal police forces, there were few allegations of abuse reported during the major operations in East Mosul. Yet, there could be problems ahead due to the complex political affiliations of the hold forces, which can skew their image and behavior as impartial providers of security, as well as their inadequate levels of training. Finally, a great risk exists that many of these forces will be drawn off for combat operations in Tal Afar and the Euphrates River Valley. During the Mosul operations, some hold forces were moved from East Mosul to participate in West Mosul operations. ISIS took advantage of the uneven security to reinfiltrate some areas and stage attacks.

Third, insufficient police forces have been prepared to take the place of the hold forces in major cities retaken from ISIS. The counter-ISIS coalition has supported efforts to recall, recruit, and train security forces, including police. The police forces trained by the Coalition amounted to 13,000 as of March 2017. According to data supplied by the Combined Joint Task Force for Operation Inherent Resolve, the additional 12,000 police forces it estimated would be needed to permanently secure the city would not be trained for another 18 months. The Coalition's police-training program had previously been accelerated through the provision of additional international trainers, but even this increased training capacity was inadequate in that it would require hold forces to stay in place for many months. Given that these same forces would likely be required for military operations in other parts of Iraq, the prospect of a dangerous gap in security in cleared areas appeared significant. In addition, many of the tribal and police forces received very brief training, so there will also be a requirement for additional training of these lightly trained forces.

Enabling the Resumption of City Life

The resumption of city life in Mosul and the return of the displaced to their homes depend on factors related to city administration: public services, infrastructure, housing, and the economy.

Under ISIS, public services broke down and infrastructure was destroyed in the fighting, with particular effects on public utilities, health care, and education. Military operations further destroyed electricity and water infrastructure; while temporary operations were under way to provide water in East Mosul, greater rebuilding will be needed. Three-quarters of Mosul's hospital space has been destroyed, as were many clinics. About half of Mosul's children were out of school; many students have been traumatized and indoctrinated.

A significant amount of infrastructure in Mosul was destroyed, both by ISIS during the occupation and by Coalition forces during the campaign to liberate Mosul. To rebuild infrastructure, the United Nations Development Programme (UNDP) operated two stabilization funds that worked with local notables to determine priorities for rebuilding; power, water, hospitals, and schools had been prioritized. The World Bank has worked elsewhere in Iraq on funding public infrastructure destroyed by fighting and stood by to finance infrastructure in Mosul.

Housing considerations will be a key problem during stabilization in Mosul for several reasons: the short supply of housing, the potential for improperly serviced neighborhoods to serve as incubators of radicalization, and the property ownership disputes that are likely to arise from ISIS's sale of property and destruction of ownership records.

Mosul's economy declined under ISIS. They looted the central bank, and many businesses closed. Unemployment, inflation, and poverty rose. Many farmers stopped working because ISIS required them to sell at low, extortive prices. Two main areas of the city economy are important for immediate stabilization: markets (for goods required for daily needs, particularly food) and jobs (as Mosul's civil service salaries were cut off from Baghdad, and many factories that provided employment were destroyed).

Governance and Political Reconciliation

Two main issues relate to the post-ISIS stabilization effort at both the local and national levels: building effective governing capacity, also known as governance, and resolving the sectarian and ethnic conflict that threatens to make Iraq a permanently failed state. The ISIS threat was rooted in the larger Iraqi political conflict that has bedeviled the country since Saddam Hussein was overthrown by the U.S. intervention in 2003. The majority of ISIS fighters were drawn from Iraq's Sunni population, though many foreign fighters joined ISIS's ranks at all levels. ISIS or its successor is likely to gain traction in Sunni areas if the long-standing grievances, core issues surrounding the division of power and the architecture of the state in Iraq, and local desires for self-governance and quality of life are not resolved.

Representative and competent government is needed in Ninewa Province, and the future boundaries and structure of the province must be ascertained. Governing capacity will need to be increased and officials with ISIS-related criminal behavior removed.

Iraq's Article 45, Law 21, the Provincial Power Act of 2013, devolved the functions of eight ministries to provincial governments. The theory was that local government could be more responsive to citizens' needs, and the closer the government was to the people, the more they would support their government. However, implementation of this law has been slow, and the United States Agency for International Development (USAID) program supporting it is set to terminate.

Mending the social fabric of Ninewa and other war-torn provinces will be required. In addition to a national-level dialogue, grassroots efforts are needed as well. A handful of successful local reconciliation efforts (such as those run by UNDP and the U.S. Institute of Peace [USIP]) could be usefully supported and scaled up.

Multiple officials believed that the establishment of ongoing national-level talks and confidence-building measures was needed between Sunnis and Shias, as well as between the Iraqi government and KRG. Yet efforts to date had failed because of political dynamics. In recent years, the United States has been working quietly behind the scenes, unwilling to put more visible political capital into the project of national reconciliation. But the advent of a new U.S. administration forces the issue of what the new U.S. policy will be.

Recommendations

This study presents 14 urgent action items to remedy gaps we identified in the immediate humanitarian response in Mosul, the most pressing and foundational stabilization needs, the critical requirements for establishing a sustained approach to governance and reconciliation, and crosscutting administrative issues. As noted previously, this is not an exhaustive catalog of needs or shortfalls in the Iraqi and international response. Rather, these action items represent the RAND study team's short list of those essential and urgent priorities without which stability and reconciliation cannot gain traction and eventually succeed. We recognize, furthermore, that in circumstances such as this, after 15 years of war, the best cannot be the enemy of the good, and partial gains are needed in the short term to create momentum and confidence that Iraq can one day construct the peace that its people deserve.

The recommendations include actions to be taken by the Iraqi government, as well as actions to be taken by the international coalition and international organizations that are supporting the government. Recommendations are for both local and national actions, for the following reasons:

1. Stabilizing Mosul and Ninewa Province requires addressing residents' concerns about national-level policies and inclusivity, as well as the purely local issues. Stabilization cannot be achieved locally without actions at the national level.
2. Given its dominant role in a centralized system, the Baghdad government will have to take actions to address both the Mosul-specific needs and the broader issues that gave rise to the conflict.
3. As the largest Sunni-majority city, Mosul serves as a microcosm for the broader task of Iraq-wide stabilization. The issues identified largely pertain to all five conflict-affected provinces.

The Humanitarian Response (0–3 Months)

1. **Address acute food, water, and medical shortages.** The life-or-death issues for Iraqis in Ninewa Province are insufficient food, water, and health care. The Iraqi government and international community must move quickly to address these critical deficits in the humanitarian response.
2. **Regularize screening and freedom of movement for IDPs.** Both the United Nations and the United States have acknowledged that international norms are not being observed for displaced civilians in some camps, particularly those run by the KRG. The KRG should immediately allow freedom of movement for displaced civilians and cease holding their government documents as a means to keep them in camps. Reuniting families should become a top priority.
3. **Promulgate and begin to implement a safe IDP return policy.** Although the UN and Iraqi government developed a detailed humanitarian response plan, an equally detailed plan for the return of the over three million IDPs is lacking. The Iraqi Department of Displacement and Migration should draw up a comprehensive plan with resources and metrics for implementation.
4. **Expand the scope and pace of explosive hazard mitigation.** Demining currently is focused on and funded only for critical infrastructure and services. Greatly increased funding and training of Iraqis for this task is required to make cities habitable and promote the early return of civilians.

Expanded Stabilization (0–6 Months)

5. **Ensure adequate hold forces in cleared areas.** Mosul's 1.2 million people will require a hold force of 60,000 troops to keep the peace, establish checkpoints, and prevent looting and reprisals. It is important to ensure that these forces are not drawn off elsewhere for other operations.
6. **Double throughput of police training.** The pace of police training should be increased by 100 percent to produce the needed number of police in 9 months

rather than 18 months. Additional training will be required for lightly trained forces that will be incorporated into the permanent police force.

7. **Restore public services and establish a process to resolve property disputes.** Resuming vital public services, enabling people to work to support their families, and beginning a process to enable people to return to their homes will be key to civilian returns, allowing those in Mosul to resume their lives and preventing an additional round of conflict over basic needs.
8. **Improve confidence in the Ninewa government.** The Iraqi prime minister should immediately convene a broadly representative council of Ninewa citizens to establish a timetable for creating an inclusive, accountable, and effective provincial government.

Helping the Iraqi Government Develop Good Governance and Political Reconciliation (0–12 Months)

9. **Implement decentralization law.** Decentralization efforts, including the Governance Strengthening Project—Taqadum funded by USAID (which concludes in September 2017), the UN Local Area Development Program, and the World Bank fiscal decentralization program, should be continued in order to support full implementation of the decentralization law passed by the Iraqi parliament. Eight ministries are to be decentralized, and implementation is under way but still incomplete. Concrete steps to empower provincial governments will support and energize national reconciliation efforts.
10. **Improve public finance and public management.** Creating an Iraqi government office that manages stabilization projects, as well as prioritizing USAID and World Bank programs that build Iraqi governing capacity through the training and monitoring of public finance and public management, will increase service delivery and public confidence levels. Performance standards should be incorporated into all funding.
11. **Expand and coordinate local reconciliation projects.** Local projects to resolve conflicts and increase social cohesion are important complements to a national-level reconciliation effort. An increase should be made in the amount of stabilization funding devoted to local-level projects, including the current UNDP plan for a media campaign, civil society gatherings, and a memory project to document the abuses and atrocities committed during the war.
12. **Jump-start national reconciliation with a road map and a Group of Friends.** The United States should take the lead in forming a Group of Friends to provide high-level support for the construction of a road map for national reconciliation in Iraq. Key components are guarantees of security, revenues, amnesty for those who have not committed crimes, a justice and accountability effort for criminals, and resettlement aid for Sunnis. Multiyear funding of the Strategic Framework Agreement should be tied to the creation of such a road map.

Crosscutting

13. **Accelerate stabilization funding.** The formal stabilization programs, Funding Facility for Immediate Stabilization (FFIS) and Funding Facility for Extended Stabilization (FFES), are not fully funded. In addition, FFIS is designed for projects of six months' duration or less. Given the magnitude of destruction in Iraq, a more extensive stabilization effort needs to be designed and funded.
14. **Improve efficiency and tracking of donor funding.** One central office should be given responsibility for tracking all pledges and contributions, so that a complete and transparent accounting of stabilization funds is publicly available. To the degree that the shortfall in funding is due to skepticism that the money is spent for the intended purposes, this issue can be most effectively addressed through increased transparency and accountability.

Acknowledgments

The authors would like to thank those who were interviewed for the study, providing valuable insights toward the analysis.

From the Iraqi government, these included Nawfal Hamadi al-Sultan, governor of Ninewa Province; General Anwer Amin, Iraqi air force chief; Ambassador Lukman Faily, former Iraqi ambassador to the United States; Jaber al-Jaberi, senior adviser to Speaker of the Council of Representatives; Brigadier General Tahseen Ibrahim, spokesman for the Iraq Ministry of Defense; National Security Service official Saeed al-Jaishy; Saad Maan, Ministry of Interior director general; Sabah al-Nouri of the Counter-Terrorism Center; Ali Sindi, minister of planning of the Kurdistan Regional Government (KRG) of Iraq; Kareem Sinjari, KRG minister of interior; Nawzad Hadi Mawlood, governor of Erbil Province; Hayder Mustafa Saaid, director general, development coordination and cooperation, KRG Ministry of Planning; and Hoshang Mohamed, director general, KRG Ministry of Interior, Joint Crisis Coordination Centre.

From the United Nations agencies and other multilateral organizations, these included Lise Grande, deputy special representative of the secretary general, resident coordinator, humanitarian coordinator, and resident representative of the United Nations Development Programme (UNDP) in Iraq; Colin Lake, senior coordination adviser, Office of the Deputy Special Representative of the Secretary General; Vincent Gule, protection officer, United Nations High Commission for Refugees (UNHCR); Precillar Moyo, UNHCR; Monica Noro, UNHCR; Andrew Barash, UNHCR; Carolina Mateos, UNHCR; Peter Hawkins, United Nations Children's Fund (UNICEF); Sultan Hajiyev, deputy country director of programme and operations, UNDP, Iraq; Fanie DuToit, consultant on reconciliation, UNDP; Erfan Ali, head of the Iraq Programme, United Nations Human Settlements Programme (UN-Habitat); Manoj Mathew, acting head of the United Nations Assistance Mission for Iraq Office of Political Affairs; Barbara Rijks, head of office, Erbil, International Organization for Migration (IOM) in Iraq; Altaf Musani, representative to Iraq, World Health Organization (WHO); Aamr Bebany, WHO; Mohammad Hamasha, WHO; and Robert Bou Jaoude, representative to Iraq, World Bank.

From the U.S. military, these included General Joseph L. Votel, commander, U.S. Central Command; Colonel James "Jay" Wolff, senior adviser, Counter Terrorism Service Office of Security Cooperation–Iraq; Colonel Ian Rice, Tribal Engagement Coordination Cell; and Major Kareem Fernandez, Tribal Engagement Coordination Cell.

U.S. diplomatic and assistance officials included Ambassador (ret.) Ryan Crocker; Ambassador (ret.) Charles Ries; Miriam Estrin, policy director, Office of the Special Presidential Envoy for the Global Coalition to Counter ISIS, U.S. Department of State; Henry Haggard, acting consul general, U.S. Consulate in Erbil; Patricia Aguilero, U.S. Department of State, Bureau of Population, Refugees, and Migration; Melanie Anderton, U.S. Department of State; Neil W. Hopp, U.S. Department of State; Stephanie Williams, deputy chief of mission, U.S. Embassy in Iraq; Mona Yacoubian, deputy assistant administrator, USAID Middle East Bureau (and colleagues); Brooke Isham, mission director, USAID; William Patterson, deputy mission director, USAID; Joseph P. Tritschler, planning coordinator, USAID's Office of Foreign Disaster Assistance (OFDA); Dianna Long, program officer, OFDA; J. Michael Nehrbass, technical chief/director of governance and economic opportunities, USAID Iraq; Ronald Mortenson, USAID/OFDA, Iraq Disaster Assistance Response Team leader; John Underriner, senior coordinator, Office of Refugees and IDP Affairs, U.S. Embassy in Iraq; Sylvia Curran, political counselor, U.S. Embassy in Iraq; Ned O'Brien, political officer, U.S. Embassy in Iraq; Kris Clark, political officer, U.S. Embassy in Iraq; and Matthew Weiller, counselor for political military affairs, U.S. Embassy in Iraq.

Nongovernmental organization officials and others included Eskandar Saleh, public relations officer, Barzani Charity Foundation; Sanaa Ibrahim, public relations officer, Barzani Charity Foundation; Hardin Lang, Center for American Progress; Daniel Benaim, Center for American Progress; Cameron Berkuti, chief of party, Chemonics International, Governance Strengthening Project—Taqadum; Noor Zandana, technical adviser, iMMAP; Kathy Keary, grants and liaison manager, Mine Action Group International; Lawk Ahmad, Iraq country director, Qandil; Father Omar, director, Herssham Camp in Erbil; Harith al-Qarawee, Iraqi scholar; Hala Sarraf, director, Iraqi Health Access Organization; and Andrew Lustig, president, Global Outreach Doctors.

Coalition officials included Brigadier General David Anderson, Canadian Armed Forces; and Christofer Burger, deputy consul general, consulate general of the Federal Republic of Germany, Erbil.

The study authors would also like to thank Seth Jones, the director of the International Security and Defense Policy Center at the RAND Corporation, for his quality assurance reviews. And we thank Krishna Kumar, director of labor and population at RAND, and Howard Shatz, senior economist at RAND, for their insightful comments during the peer review process for this report. The authors thank the team members who contributed to the literature reviews for the study, particularly the case studies on Fallujah, Ramadi, and Tikrit: Ilana Blum and Sarah Weilant. We thank Diane Egelhoff for her work on the references.

CHAPTER ONE

Introduction

Study Purpose

Military operations to defeat the Islamic State of Iraq and Syria (ISIS), as well as the humanitarian and stabilization response to help civilians affected by ISIS in Iraq, have created notable successes. Yet there exists a significant risk that military victory will dislodge ISIS, only for Iraq to fall into an extended period of destabilization and human suffering due to inadequate short- and long-term measures to address the challenge of some 3 million remaining internally displaced persons (IDPs) and unstable situations in Iraq's cities. Another phase of upheaval in Iraq would be tragic for the Iraqi people, could destabilize other countries in the Middle East, may lead to another round of displaced people fleeing to other Middle Eastern countries or onward to Europe, and would once again draw in the Iraqi and American troops who have fought to bring peace. That would be a sad outcome for the people of Iraq and for all those who have given their lives, expended resources, and made great efforts to create a better future for Iraq.

The fate of Mosul in particular is critical for the ultimate outcome of the effort to defeat ISIS in Iraq. Mosul is Iraq's second-largest city, its largest Sunni-majority city, and the largest city held by ISIS. Mosul is the site of the last major urban battle in Iraq against ISIS—what happens afterward will be the bellwether for the next phase of Iraq's trajectory: more war or the beginning of a way out. At the same time, stabilization of Mosul at the local level depends on concomitant steps to address problems at the national level—particularly in security, governance, and reconciliation. In that sense, Mosul serves as an important microcosm in considering needed steps for all of those parts of Iraq that have been affected by ISIS.

Therefore, this accumulating crisis and the eventual implications call for those involved to take part in urgent planning, address challenges, and build on successes. This report focuses on the aftermath of the major combat operations in Mosul and the critical requirements for achieving lasting stability, which include humanitarian assistance, security, public services, and governance in the conflict zones. The issues identified here also mirror the broader national requirements for nationwide stability, reconstruction, and reconciliation. While the report focuses on Mosul, it also aims to offer insight on the efforts to bring about the safe return of all of Iraq's displaced civilians and provide assistance to the estimated 10 million people—one-third of Iraq's population—who have been directly affected by the war. Indeed, as Iraqi prime minister Haider al-Abadi said about the defeat of ISIS, "the difficult part will be after liberation."[1]

The report should be helpful to planning efforts by the United States, the Iraqi central government, Iraqi subnational governments (particularly the Ninewa provincial and Kurdistan Regional governments), and the international humanitarian assistance community, which is playing a significant role through the United Nations, the Global Coalition to Counter ISIS, and bilateral efforts. This report makes a unique contribution by drawing on timely primary source materials from key leaders of government, military, and aid agencies with leadership responsibilities related to these issues; combining humanitarian and security perspectives; and offering recommendations that are crucial for the successful stabilization of Mosul and the rest of the country. The recommendations target the improvement of the most critical aspects of programs and policies for humanitarian assistance and stabilization, thus ensuring that the campaign to defeat ISIS is ultimately successful.

Approach

This study reviewed the situation and needs in Mosul and analyzed where gaps or problems existed through a literature review, case studies of other liberated Iraqi cities, interviews in the United States, and fieldwork in Iraq. The study considered circumstances through April 2017, although we do include some summary statistics through July 2017. Through the phases of our research, we considered the following factors: politics (both national and local), administration (roles of main actors and status of public services), security (policing, hold forces, and explosive remnants of war [ERW]), economics (infrastructure, utilities, jobs, consumer goods markets, and rebuilding opportunities), and conditions for civilian returns home (enabling factors, risks to civilians, and unmet needs).

- **Literature and data review:** We reviewed relevant literature and data, including publicly available reports and media about circumstances in Mosul, conditions of displaced persons in Iraq, programs and responses, and military strategy. We drew on extensive databases updated weekly and monthly by the UN and key implementing partners, particularly the International Organization for Migration (IOM) Displacement Tracking Matrix and the United Nations Human Settlements Programme (UN-Habitat) reports and visualizations. We collaborated with iMMAP Iraq to compile a current map of explosive remnants of war.

1 *Rudaw*, "Abadi Promises Mosul Leaders Decentralized Governance After Liberation," July 26, 2016. As of April 10, 2017: http://rudaw.net/english/middleeast/iraq/260720161.

- **Case studies:** We researched past experiences with stabilization in three Iraqi cities (Tikrit, Ramadi, and Fallujah) that had been liberated from ISIS, as well as efforts to return residents who had been displaced from these cities. The purpose of these case studies was to identify and compare areas of chronic shortfalls, successful efforts to address them, and lessons learned. Tikrit, the capital of Salah al-Din Province, was taken by ISIS in June 2014 and retaken by Iraq in March 2015. Ramadi, the capital of Anbar Province, was taken by ISIS in May 2015 and retaken by Iraq in December 2015. Fallujah, also in Anbar Province, was taken by ISIS in January 2014 and retaken by Iraq in June 2016. Their experiences postliberation provided rich lessons about stabilization and civilian returns, particularly related to demining, rubble removal, grassroots reconciliation efforts, the use of cash grants for markets to resume quickly, the need for professionalism among hold forces and police, and public communication to displaced persons about their return home.
- **Interviews in Iraq and the United States:** We conducted interviews with the major stakeholders in the humanitarian and stabilization effort in Iraq, including (1) U.S. civilian and military officials, (2) Iraqi government and military officials (including the Kurdistan Regional Government [KRG]) in both Baghdad and Erbil, (3) UN officials in all key UN agencies, (4) officials in international and Iraqi nongovernmental organizations (NGOs), and (5) Coalition members. Key questions asked of interviewees regarded the following: (1) assessment of humanitarian conditions and types and amounts of assistance and aid being provided, (2) assessment of the provision of public services and security, (3) perception and documentation of unmet needs, (4) policies and procedures governing humanitarian and stabilization programs and services, and (5) programs and plans to address political grievances and lack of governance capacity or capability. Stakeholders were also asked to prioritize needs and recommend remedial or additional measures to address identified gaps.

  To comply with RAND's human subjects protection guidelines for this project, the research team conducted interviews on a nonattribution basis to protect the interview subjects from risks that disclosure of their identities might entail. Public statements by officials were not included in these restrictions. Interview subjects were not asked to represent their organizations; they were asked only to speak for themselves.
- **Site visits to key locations in Iraq:** We visited military bases (Qayarah and Hammam Al-Alil) and IDP camps (Hersham Camp in Erbil and Khazer I and II Camps outside Mosul) to assess conditions there. Camp officials and NGO workers were interviewed to determine the number of residents, the types of aid and services provided, and the procedures and conditions governing the camps. The researchers also surveyed the physical conditions of the camps and residents.
- **Gap analysis:** After recognizing important steps and progress to date, we analyzed the major gaps in the humanitarian response, security, city functions, and governance and reconciliation.

- **Development of criteria for recommendations:** We developed three criteria to select recommendations, focusing on issues that were (1) most urgent, (2) most fundamental to enduring success, or (3) technical prerequisites for other actions to occur.
- **Key findings and recommendations:** Drawing on our previous steps, our analysis took a multisectoral approach: we examined the interaction among the military, humanitarian, political, and economic aspects in order to frame issues holistically for policymakers. Although our focus was on Mosul, many of the issues identified are national-level ones as well, or they rely on national-level action to resolve. While the literature addressing the national-level issues in Iraq is crowded, our approach considered how the Mosul-particular and national issues are connected, and specifically what was essential for near-term progress in order to tightly scope the focus for policymakers. We received overwhelming response from interviewees articulating this connection.

An Overview of Mosul Before, During, and After ISIS

Beginning in 2014, ISIS captured a third of Iraq's territory, mainly in the Ninewa, Anbar, Salah al-Din, Diyala, and Kirkuk Provinces. In 2009, Ninewa Province had an estimated 2.8–3.3 million people, including its capital city, Mosul.[2] Figure 1.1 depicts a map of Iraq, with Ninewa Province highlighted.

Before ISIS took it in 2014, Mosul was a prominent commercial center and was estimated to have had 1.5–2 million people. A city straddling the banks of the Tigris River (see Figure 1.2), West Mosul is home to the older part of the city, and East Mosul is home to the newer parts.

After the fall of Mosul and other parts of Ninewa to ISIS, 1.3 million people from the province fled their homes and moved elsewhere in Ninewa or to other Iraqi provinces, becoming IDPs.[3] In addition to displaced Sunnis, many who fled in 2014 were minorities (such as Christians, Yazidis, Shabaks, or Turkmen) or those who opposed ISIS. Indeed, the Yazidis were particularly targeted as the victims of atrocities, mass murders, the enslavement of women, and the destruction of heritage.

---

[2] IOM: Iraq Mission, "Ninewa Governorate Profile, May 2015," 2015. As of March 27, 2017: http://iomiraq.net/reports/ninewa-governorate-profile-may-2015; Inter-Agency Information and Analysis Unit and United Nations Office for the Coordination of Humanitarian Affairs (UNOCHA), *Governorate Profile for Ninewa*, December 2010.

[3] IOM: Iraq Mission, "Displacement Tracking Matrix | DTM," UN Migration Agency, March 16, 2017a. Time series October 2016–April 1, 2017. As of March 27, 2017: http://iraqdtm.iom.int/IDPsML.aspx.

Figure 1.1
Map of Iraq

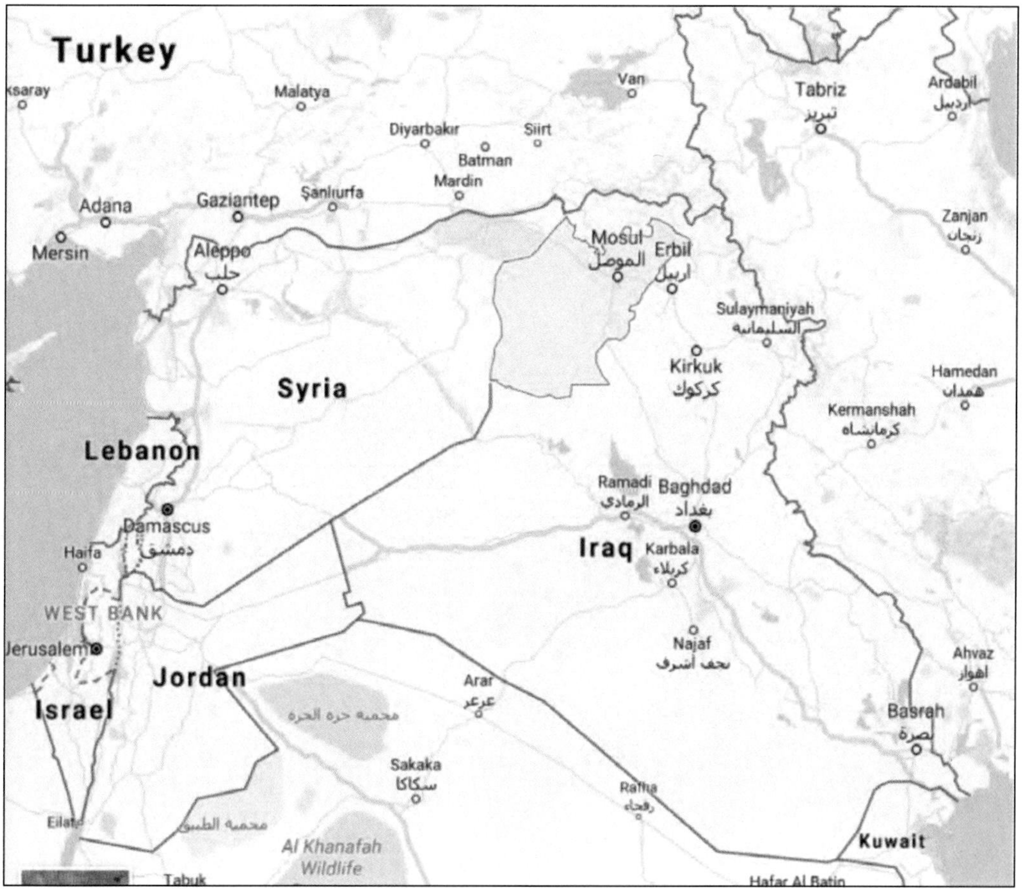

SOURCE: Google Maps.
RAND *RR2076-1.1*

Under ISIS, Mosul experienced a severe humanitarian crisis and economic decline.[4] Basic services collapsed. Unemployment and poverty increased. ISIS enforced strict social controls, used people as human shields, forced children to become suicide bombers, destroyed cultural heritage, confiscated properties, and looted the central bank. The Iraqi central government cut off salaries to public employees in Mosul so that ISIS could not extort money from them.

---

4 Terrence McCoy, "ISIS Just Stole $425 Million, Iraqi Governor Says, and Became the 'World's Richest Terrorist Group,'" *Washington Post*, June 12, 2014; Megan O'Toole, "How Will Mosul Rise from the Ashes of Battle?," *Al Jazeera*, November 12, 2016. As of March 27, 2017: http://www.aljazeera.com/indepth/features/2016/11/mosul-rise-ashes-battle-161112100900149.html.

Figure 1.2
Map of the City of Mosul

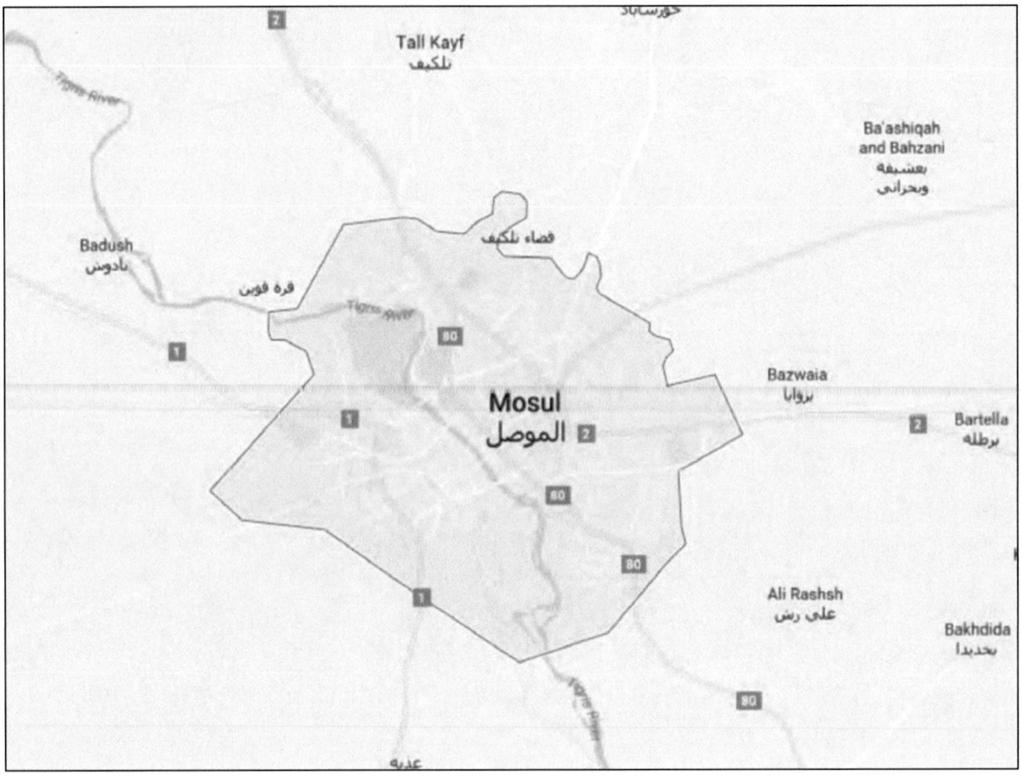

SOURCE: Google Maps.
RAND *RR2076-1.2*

By June 2016, Iraqi Security Forces backed by U.S. and Coalition airpower had liberated most of the territories held by ISIS, including our case study cities of Tikrit, Ramadi, and Fallujah. All told, ISIS's brutal rule, as well as the fighting to liberate territories from it, led to the displacement of 5.3 million Iraqis from their homes.[5] By July 2017, 2 million civilians had returned to their homes in liberated areas, but 3.3 million remained displaced.[6]

---

[5] IOM Iraq, "Displacement Tracking Matrix: IDP Locations & Population, January 2014–May 26, 2016," 2016a. As of March 27, 2017: http://reliefweb.int/sites/reliefweb.int/files/resources/Round46_Map_Location_Population_2016_May_26_IOM_DTM.pdf.

[6] IOM Iraq, "Displacement Tracking Matrix: Factsheet #36—Mosul Operations from 17 October to 16 July," 2017. As of July 7, 2017: http://iraqdtm.iom.int/Downloads/DTM%20Emergency%20Tracking/Mosul%20Crisis/1-Mosul%20Operations%20Factsheets/DTM%20ET%20Mosul%20Operations%20Factsheet%20%2336.pdf.

Operations began to retake parts of Ninewa Province in October 2016. As part of Operation Inherent Resolve, which aimed to retake the parts of Iraq that ISIS had conquered, the campaign to retake Ninewa was called "We're Coming, Ninewa." By January 2017, Iraqi forces and the Coalition had retaken East Mosul. During that wave of fighting, 182,000 people were displaced from East Mosul and its surroundings, receiving shelter in pre-prepared camps. Of these, 70,000 returned to their homes by March 2017. An estimated 300,000 people remained in liberated East Mosul. After the military operations concluded in East Mosul, city life began to resume quickly, with markets and schools opening. Yet much remained to be done to repair the human and infrastructure damage inflicted.

Operations to retake West Mosul began in February 2017. Up to 750,000 people remained in ISIS-occupied West Mosul at the beginning of the fighting,[7] living among 12,000–15,000 ISIS fighters and struggling with acute food and water insecurity. The fighting for West Mosul had displaced an additional 153,000 people by late March 2017.[8] Total displacement from both East and West Mosul, after accounting for returns, was 270,000 by March 2017.[9] By July 2017, a total of over a million people had been displaced by the fighting in Mosul, and some 200,00 had returned, leaving net displacement at 822,000. From the beginning of the Mosul offensive in October 2016 until March 2017, 774 Iraqi troops were killed, with 4,600 wounded.[10]

Humanitarian Assistance and Stabilization

This study focuses on the initial steps needed for Mosul to begin to recover after military operations, including the humanitarian response and stabilization. The research design recognizes that these activities are part of an overlapping continuum. Mosul, and Iraq more generally, faces a long road to fully recover from the destruction and trauma caused by ISIS, with multiple steps: military operations, the humanitarian response, stabilization, reconstruction, and development.

---

7 UN News Centre, "Humanitarian Crisis in Mosul Could Outlive Iraqi Military Operations, Senior UN Official Warns," United Nations, 2017. As of March 27, 2017: http://www.un.org/apps/news/story.asp?NewsID=55948#.WJtkEBiZMmJ.

8 UN Refugee Agency, "UNHCR Mosul Weekly Protection Update," United Nations, March 11–17, 2017. Time series reports October 2016–April 2017. As of March 27, 2017: http://reliefweb.int/sites/reliefweb.int/files/resources/UNHCR%20Mosul%20Weekly%20Protection%20Update%2011-17%20Mar.pdf.

9 IOM: Iraq Mission, "Iraq Mission: Displacement Tracking Matrix | DTM," UN Migration Agency, March 23, 2017b. As of March 27, 2017: http://iraqdtm.iom.int/EmergencyTracking.aspx.

10 Patrick Osgood, Rawaz Tahir, and *Iraq Oil Report* staff, "IS Use of Human Shields Complicated Mosul Offensive," *Iraq Oil Report*, March 31, 2017. As of March 31, 2017: http://www.iraqoilreport.com/news/use-human-shields-complicates-mosul-offensive-21900/.

What are humanitarian assistance and stabilization, and what do they include? Humanitarian assistance is short-term help that "saves lives, alleviates suffering, and maintains human dignity"[11] through the provision of shelter; food and water, hygiene (WASH); and urgent health care. Stabilization is the restoration of living conditions to such an extent that society functions at a basic level and can embark on longer-term reconstruction and development activities.[12] The U.S. government's "stability sectors" include security, justice and reconciliation, foreign humanitarian assistance and social well-being, governance and participation, and economic stabilization and infrastructure.[13] The UK government views stabilization as having three activities: the protection of political actors, the political system, and the population; the promotion, consolidation, and strengthening of political processes; and preparation for longer-term recovery.[14] Stabilization is often described as a set of postconflict activities that are needed between humanitarian action and development. While nomenclature in this field varies, the essential distinction between humanitarian aid (food, water, shelter, sanitation, and health care) and stabilization is that the former is based strictly on need, and stabilization is an inherently political activity in that the assistance is intended to bolster governing capacity, the ability of a government to deliver services, and hence the legitimacy of that government.

Stakeholders and Programs for Humanitarian and Stabilization Response

The principal actors engaged in the humanitarian response and stabilization in Iraq are the Iraqi government (including the central government, as well as subnational governments), the U.S. and other donor governments, and the United Nations system and its implementing partners.

The central Iraqi government provides direction and coordination, with the prime minister's office leading coordination on stabilization with the provinces impacted by ISIS and the United Nations. Iraqi subnational governments, including for Ninewa Province, Anbar Province, and the Kurdistan Region, play key roles in providing human-

[11] Organisation for Economic Cooperation and Development, "Humanitarian Assistance," 2016. As of March 27, 2017: http://www.oecd.org/dac/stats/humanitarian-assistance.htm.

[12] The U.S. military defines *stabilization* as "the process by which military and nonmilitary actors collectively apply various instruments of national power to address drivers of conflict, foster host-nation resiliencies, and create conditions that enable sustainable peace and security." Joint Publication 1-02. *Department of Defense Dictionary of Military and Associated Terms*, as amended through March 15, 2012, Washington, D.C.: Joint Chiefs of Staff, 2012.

[13] Chairman of the Joint Chiefs of Staff, "Joint Publication 3-07: Stability," United States Department of Defense, August 3, 2016. As of March 27, 2017: http://www.dtic.mil/doctrine/new_pubs/jp3_07.pdf.

[14] Stabilisation Unit, "The UK Government's Approach to Stabilisation," UK Foreign and Commonwealth Office, UK Ministry of Defence, and UK Department for International Development, May 2014. As of March 27, 2017: http://www.sclr.stabilisationunit.gov.uk/attachments/article/520/TheUKApproachtoStabilisationMay2014.pdf.

itarian assistance and security and deciding on specific projects to be implemented by UN agencies. Iraq's Ministry of Displacement and Migration is responsible for managing the needs of IDPs. While expectations had been that the central Iraqi government would fund stabilization, Iraq's financial crisis impedes its ability to do so. In Iraq's oil-dependent economy, nearly the entire government budget derives from export revenues; the decline in oil prices in 2014 cut Iraq's government revenue. ISIS's rise in 2014 demanded increased defense expenditures and cut off regional trade routes. This combination created a financial crisis.

There are 20 donor countries involved in humanitarian and stabilization efforts in Iraq. The United States is the largest donor. It has spent $1.1 billion in humanitarian aid in Iraq since 2014, and it pledged an additional $513 million in the 2016–2017 fiscal year for humanitarian efforts in Mosul.[15] The United States provides funding for United Nations agencies and implementing NGO partners to manage humanitarian assistance and stabilization. The Coalition Working Group on Stabilization (within the Coalition) is cochaired by the United Arab Emirates and Germany. Estimated humanitarian response needs for Iraq total $4.5 billion.[16] In 2016, the Coalition raised $1.4 to $2.3 billion for humanitarian and stabilization action in Iraq for liberated areas; this money is managed by the UN system.[17] Actual new commitments were unclear, as senior UN and Western diplomats noted the lack of a centralized picture, with incidences of double counting of donations across funds. Donors were not considering funding for reconstruction, but those costs certainly would run into the billions of dollars given the level of destruction of major cities.

The United Nations system supports the Iraqi government in leading both the humanitarian and stabilization responses. The two efforts are managed differently, with the humanitarian response a traditional "coordination" effort of multiple actors, and the stabilization response administered by the United Nations Development Programme (UNDP). Most donor assistance is channeled through UN agencies and international NGOs.

Humanitarian assistance is managed by a complex architecture involving 18 UN agencies, 79 international NGOs, and 54 national NGOs.[18] The United Nations Office for the Coordination of Humanitarian Affairs (UNOCHA) leads the "cluster system"

---

15 "Press Conference by SPE [Special Presidential Envoy] Mcgurk in Baghdad, Iraq," U.S. Department of State, October 25, 2016. As of March 28, 2017: https://2009-2017.state.gov/s/seci/263568.htm.

16 United Nations Humanitarian Country Team, "2016 Humanitarian Response Plan: Iraq," UNOCHA, December 2015. As of March 27, 2017: http://reliefweb.int/sites/reliefweb.int/files/resources/final_iraq_2016_hrp.pdf.

17 "Update on Campaign Against ISIL: Special Briefing by Brett Mcgurk, Special Presidential Envoy for the Global Coalition to Counter ISIL," U.S. Department of State, October 6, 2016. As of March 28, 2017: https://2009-2017.state.gov/r/pa/prs/ps/2016/10/262934.htm.

18 Internal Displacement Monitoring Centre, "Iraq: IDPs Caught Between a Rock and a Hard Place as Displacement Crisis Deepens," June 30, 2015. As of March 27, 2017: http://www.internal-displacement.org/middle-east-and-north-africa/iraq/2015/iraq-idps-caught-between-a-rock-and-a-hard-place-as-displacement-crisis-deepens.

that organizes the humanitarian response in Mosul, with the following clusters: protection; food security; health; water, sanitation, and hygiene; shelter and nonfood items; camp coordination and camp management; education; emergency livelihoods and social cohesion; the rapid-response mechanism; emergency telecommunications; logistics; and common services and coordination.[19] In addition to UNOCHA, the lead UN agencies in the humanitarian response are the United Nations High Commission for Refugees (UNHCR), the United Nations Children's Fund (UNICEF), IOM, the World Food Programme (WFP), UN-Habitat, and the World Health Organization (WHO). International NGOs, national NGOs, and private-sector companies implement programs on behalf of UN agencies and bilateral donors.

The UNDP's Funding Facility for Immediate Stabilization (FFIS) in Iraq is the main vehicle for stabilization activities supported by the international community. The FFIS is strictly bounded in terms of timeline: projects must be completed within six months of initiation. As of its October 2016 quarterly report, the FFIS had received $95 million in funding. The FFIS established four categories under which all projects must fall: light infrastructure rehabilitation, livelihoods support, capacity building, and community reconciliation. Funds have primarily been expended in the first two categories. A follow-on program has also been initiated, the Funding Facility for Extended Stabilization (FFES). The FFES is intended to bridge the FFIS and reconstruction, covering up to three years and requesting $800 million through 2018.

Organization of This Report

Following this introduction, Chapter Two describes humanitarian circumstances, responses, and needs for people from Mosul: those inside East and West Mosul, IDPs who fled the military operations, and IDPs who fled ISIS in 2014–2015. Chapter Three assesses the most urgent security needs following combat operations: the removal of ERW, temporary hold forces after Mosul is cleared of ISIS fighters, and competent police. Chapter Four analyzes the key elements for the resumption of city life in Mosul: public services, infrastructure, housing, and the economy. Chapter Five analyzes local and national governance and reconciliations needs, including governance of Ninewa Province, decentralization of national public services to the provinces, local reconciliation among traumatized communities, and national reconciliation efforts. Finally, Chapter Six concludes with recommendations of urgent action items that should be addressed in the next 12 months; these concern urgent humanitarian needs, stabilization considerations, governance and political reconciliation issues, and crosscutting administrative issues.

---

[19] UNOCHA, *Mosul Flash Appeal*, July 20, 2016a. As of March 24, 2017: https://docs.unocha.org/sites/dms/Iraq/mosul_flash_appeal_final_web%20(1).pdf.

CHAPTER TWO

The Humanitarian Response

As the battle for Mosul unfolded, by July 2017, a total of over a million people from Mosul had been displaced by the military operations; some 200,000 had returned home, leaving a net displacement of 822,000. Challenges for providing aid to civilians remaining inside West Mosul were significant. In addition, the longer-term displacement of people in 2014 and 2015 by ISIS remained a challenge in terms of both meeting their immediate needs and addressing their eventual local integration, resettlement elsewhere, or return home. This chapter describes the situation of people from Mosul, the humanitarian response by the aid community, and notable needs. The population of Mosul can be divided into three categories: people inside Mosul, those who fled the offensive that started in October 2016, and the longer-term IDPs who fled ISIS in 2014 and 2015. Table 2.1 summarizes the main challenges in the humanitarian situation of these three populations, with description following.

Circumstances Inside East and West Mosul

The Situation

When plans for the military operations were under way, the Iraqi government instructed Moslawis (people from Mosul) to stay in place during the battle if they could, and flee only if necessary. This decision was highly controversial because of the risks posed to civilians staying in place and the difficulties this created for the Iraqi forces battling ISIS fighters, as they were then forced to do so among civilians. There would potentially be high casualty rates of both civilians staying in the city during the fighting and Iraqi forces retaking the city, as they could not rely as heavily on airpower. Yet Iraqi, U.S., and UN officials interviewed explained the reasoning for the instructions to stay at home.[1] By remaining in Mosul, people could avoid living in difficult camp conditions and avoid the numerous difficulties in returning home. Citizens who stayed in place would also lessen risk of being killed by ISIS on corridors out of Mosul, as had been the

[1] Interviews with Iraqi military official, UN official, KRG official, and U.S. officials in Erbil, Iraq, January 2017; telephone interview with UN official in Iraq, February 13, 2017; interview with U.S. officials in Washington, D.C., December 13, 2016; telephone interview with UN official in Iraq, February 13, 2017.

Table 2.1
Challenges in the Humanitarian Situation of People from Mosul

People Inside East and West Mosul	IDPs Generated by Offensive	IDPs Generated by ISIS in 2014–2015
Acute food insecurity	Lack of uniform screening processes	Dwindling assistance
Destruction of water supplies	Restricted freedom of movement	Poverty and high unemployment
Security barriers to the provision of aid	Family separation	Low education rates
Lack of services to address urgent health care needs	Insufficiency of camp space	Strains on host communities
	Emergency sites that serve as camps, instead of camps at international camp standards	Fears of reprisals upon return
	Lack of services for physical and mental health care	
	Barriers to leaving camps	
	Missing documentation	

case elsewhere.[2] Abandoning a city during the battle meant leaving it vulnerable to high levels of destruction, as was the case in Ramadi and Fallujah. Ramadi, for example, was heavily booby-trapped by ISIS, and further damage was inflicted by extensive use of airpower and artillery in retaking the city. The Iraqi government predicted that relying on Iraqi forces proceeding carefully house to house, rather than primarily on airpower and artillery, could potentially better protect civilians and their homes. Finally, nearby cities were already coping with strains in housing, health care, and more from accepting previous waves of IDPs.

U.S., UN, and Iraqi officials all noted that the strategy of advising civilians to stay in place, in combination with reliance on Iraqi ground operations rather than airpower, worked "better than anyone had expected" in East Mosul, although it had meant higher casualties for Iraqi forces. Indeed, in the battle for East Mosul, 500 Iraqi soldiers were killed and 3,000 wounded.[3] The 180,000 people displaced in the campaign to take East Mosul and its surroundings were far fewer than the estimated 1 million upper limit (for the entire city).

The debate over the best recourse for civilians was reopened when West Mosul was effectively closed off by approaching security forces, which bottled up the ISIS

[2] Accompanying story and video from PBS *News Hour*: Gareth Browne, "Meet the U.S. Volunteers Treating Patients at a Front Line Clinic in Mosul," *Middle East Eye*, December 18, 2016. As of March 24, 2017: http://www.middleeasteye.net/in-depth/features/meet-volunteers-front-line-clinic-mosul-1822411855.

[3] Michael R. Gordon, "U.S. Forces Play Crucial Role Against ISIS in Mosul," *New York Times*, February 26, 2017a. As of March 24, 2017: https://www.nytimes.com/2017/02/26/world/middleeast/mosul-iraq-american-military-role-islamic-state.html.

fighters and forced the battle to occur in and around the population. Many of the 12,000–15,000 ISIS fighters that remained in Iraq waged fierce battles in the narrow streets of the Old City.[4] Some 150,000 Moslawis fled the western districts in the first month of the West Mosul offensive, but most of the 750,000 residents remained in place, either trapped or unwilling to leave. Furthermore, ISIS used civilians as human shields, coercing malnourished families to live near military targets by offering food, and killing families who tried to leave. Coalition airstrikes also led to high numbers of casualties. The UN reported over 300 civilian casualties in West Mosul from its mid-February start through late March.[5]

The Response and Needs in East Mosul

Since Iraqis largely stayed in place in East Mosul, providers of humanitarian assistance sought to deliver aid quickly to liberated areas, and city street life quickly resumed. People came out of their homes, and markets reopened. The aid system began helping civilians to meet basic needs. UNICEF moved quickly to engineer the reconnection of water systems for East Mosul. Aid workers aimed to bring assistance inside the city, despite security risks. Among the major problems encountered were drinking water shortages, injured civilians, pent-up demand for health care, and the safety of aid workers as they attempted to reach populations in need. Indeed, a suicide bomber killed 4 aid workers and 23 civilians in one attack in East Mosul in December.[6]

The Response and Needs in West Mosul

Given the ongoing fighting in West Mosul in early to mid-2017, options for helping civilians trapped inside were limited. Problems with meeting basic needs—particularly food, water, and health care—became so dire that, according to one diplomat, the Coalition at one point considered a managed evacuation of civilians, despite the risk of attacks on civilians leaving the city and the lack of capacity to vet and host even greater numbers of fleeing civilians.

While food, water, and other supplies had continued to reach civilians before the offensive started, the food and water shortages became increasingly acute as the weeks went on. Those fleeing cited lack of food as the main reason they left. A UN situation assessment found shortages of food and drinking water, estimating that

---

[4] "Press Briefing by Press Secretary Josh Earnest and Special Envoy for the Global Coalition to Counter ISIL, Brett McGurk," White House: Office of the Press Secretary, December 13, 2016. As of March 24, 2017: https://obamawhitehouse.archives.gov/the-press-office/2016/12/13/press-briefing-press-secretary-josh-earnest-and-special-envoy-global.

[5] Osgood, Tahir, and *Iraq Oil Report* staff, "IS Use of Human Shields Complicated Mosul Offensive."

[6] "Mosul Battle: Triple Car Bomb Attack Kills 23 at Market," *BBC News*, December 22, 2016. As of March 28, 2017: http://www.bbc.com/news/world-middle-east-38406631.

80 percent of essential foodstuffs were unavailable.[7] The UN estimated in mid-March that a quarter of the population was down to one meal a day. Residents also reported a lack of clean drinking water (with available water often brackish) and shortages of fuel.[8] For many, sustained access to food depended on their ability to hide and horde and on their social networks for sharing.

The capacity to address health care needs, including ongoing urgent health care and trauma care, was critically inadequate, according to UN, U.S., and KRG officials.[9] Little health care was available close to the fighting because of the risks posed for health care workers, and because ISIS required existing health care facilities inside Mosul to care for wounded fighters first. A handful of health care workers, supervised by the WHO, operated trauma care services for civilians within half a mile of the battle. The Iraqi special operations forces sent their surgical staff to Ninewa to lend a hand. After immediate trauma stabilization, patients were transported to another trauma facility, operated by an NGO. During the military operations for East Mosul, most trauma cases were sent to either Erbil (some 40 miles away—a lengthy journey through multiple checkpoints) or the U.S.-funded Samaritan's Purse, a trauma facility 15 km from Mosul run by American expatriates. The governor of Erbil Province reserved three hospitals for trauma treatment for casualties of the Mosul operations. Yet there was a shortage of spaces and supplies and high demands on their few staff members, including shortages of burn specialists and anesthesiologists.[10] After learning lessons during the operations for East Mosul about the strains on trauma patients traveling through checkpoints to Erbil, and the overloading of Erbil's hospital capacity, the WHO, with Coalition funding, set up six other hospitals for field trauma from the military operations in West Mosul; the WHO health care request for lifesaving interventions in Mosul was $120 million.

Circumstances of the IDPs Generated by the Offensive

The Situation

As of mid-March 2017, an estimated 270,000 Iraqis remained displaced from Mosul and the immediate surrounding areas. While some 70,000 had returned to East Mosul, the UN predicted that an additional 250,000 people or more could be displaced from West Mosul as the fighting continued. In addition, ISIS attempts to destabilize East Mosul through bombings and other attacks could escalate and produce renewed out-

---

7 UN-Habitat, *Rapid Situation Assessment: Living Conditions on the Right Bank of Mosul*, February 2, 2017b.

8 UNICEF, "Humanitarians Fear for the 750,000 Civilians in Western Mosul," January 24, 2017a. As of March 24, 2017: https://www.unicef.org/media/media_94438.html.

9 Interviews with UN, U.S., and KRG officials in Erbil, Iraq, January 2017.

10 Telephone interview with representative of NGO operating near Mosul, April 4, 2017.

flows. Indeed by July, over a total of a million people from Mosul had displaced, with 822,000 remaining displaced.

For those who fled the operations that began in October 2016, the Iraqi government made a decision to send them to camps or "emergency sites," despite UNHCR guidance to avoid camp-based solutions because civilians can remain in them for years.[11] Interviews with Iraqi government, UN, KRG, and U.S. officials described this decision as based on two factors: (1) nearby cities were struggling to cope as they accommodated large numbers of displaced people, and (2) there was widespread distrust of the displaced population from Mosul because they had lived under ISIS for nearly three years, creating concern about their sympathies and activities and the possibility of sleeper cells.[12] Officials explained that IDPs from Mosul were "under a cloak of suspicion" as collaborators or the targets of indoctrination; there was concern about the potential impact of their presence or activities if they moved onward.[13] While these concerns could be valid for a portion of the IDPs, numerous international officials argued that it was not accurate to assume this for most of the population, as people stayed in Mosul for many reasons, including not having other places to go, not wanting to live in camps, or having elderly family members or young children who could not leave.

The principal emergency camps in the Ninewa plains, as depicted in Figure 2.1, were Hassan Sham, Khazer I, and Khazer II; in the southern flanks of Mosul, the largest camps were Hamman al-Alil and Qayarah. If IDPs had a guarantor and passed screening, then they were permitted instead to go to a community; about 85 percent of IDPs went into camps.[14]

The Response and Needs

There were three significant types of problems with the camps: protection issues, camp conditions, and challenges returning home.

Protection Issues

U.S. and UN diplomats stated that the most serious problems overall were various issues of protection.[15] The handling of IDPs prompted several major concerns: uniform screening processes were not established and conducted by official entities with proper training, particularly at informal screening points; IDPs that arrived in some

---

[11] UNHCR: The UN Refugee Agency, *UNHCR Policy on Refugee Protection and Solutions in Urban Areas*, September 2009. As of March 28, 2017: http://www.unhcr.org/4ab356ab6.pdf.

[12] Telephone interview with UN official in Iraq, February 13, 2017.

[13] Interviews with U.S. officials in Washington, D.C., in December 2016; interviews with UN, U.S., and KRG officials in Erbil, Iraq, January 2017.

[14] UNICEF, 2017a.

[15] Interview with U.S. officials in Washington, D.C., December 13, 2016; interview with UN officials in Erbil, Iraq, January 2017; telephone interview with UN official in Iraq, February 13, 2017.

Figure 2.1
Camps for IDPs from the Battle for Mosul

IRAQ: Mosul Operational Planning - Camps and Emergency Sites (15 January 2017)

Zone	Gov.	Emergency Camps	Lead Agency	Occupied	Plots Available	Additional Planned
1	Nin.	Hasansham U3	UNHCR	1,636	300	-
	Nin.	Khazer M1	MoMD	7,000	FULL	-
	Nin.	Hasansham M2 (Khazer M2)	MoMD	5,000	FULL	1,000
	Sul.	Surdesh	MoMD	-	400	-
	Nin.	Chamakor	UNHCR	-	1,008	1,392
	Nin.	Hasansham U2	UNHCR	-	Under construction	1,500
2	Nin.	Qaymawa (former Zelikan)	UNHCR	1,029	FULL	-
	Nin.	Amalla	UNHCR	-	3,032	-
	Nin.	Nargizlia 1	MoMD	1,022	1,542	-
	Nin.	Zelikan (new)	MoMD	-	Under construction	4,360
	Nin.	Nargizlia 2	MoMD	-	Under construction	4,080
	Nin.	Piran (Nargizlia 3)	IKL*	-	To be assessed	1,000
4	Nin.	Qayyarah Jad'ah 1-3	MoMD	4,000	FULL	-
	Nin.	Qayyarah Jad'ah 4	MoMD	500	FULL	1,500
	Sal.	Al-Alam 2 (MoMD)	MoMD	750	FULL	4,350
	Nin.	As Salamyiah	N.Gov**	-	Under construction	2,000
	Nin.	Hamam Al Alil	MoMD	-	Under construction	4,000
	Sal.	Al Sh'hamah	MoMD	-	Under construction	2,500
	Sal.	Olympic Stadium	UNHCR	-	Under construction	900

**Ninewa Goverment *Islamic Kurdish League

Zone	Gov.	Emergency Sites	Lead Agency	Occupied	Plots Available	Additional Planned
4	Nin.	Qayyarah Airstrip	IOM	2,860	FULL	7,140
	Nin.	Haj Ali	IOM	75	FULL	7,425
	Sal.	Basateen Al Sheuokh	UNDP	-	Under construction	2,500

Nin=Ninewa; Sul=Sulaymaniyah; Sal=Salah al-Din

Occupied:	23,872 Plots	(137,521 People[1])
Available:	6,282 Plots	(37,692 People)
Under Construction Or Planned:	45,647 Plots[2]	(273,882 People)

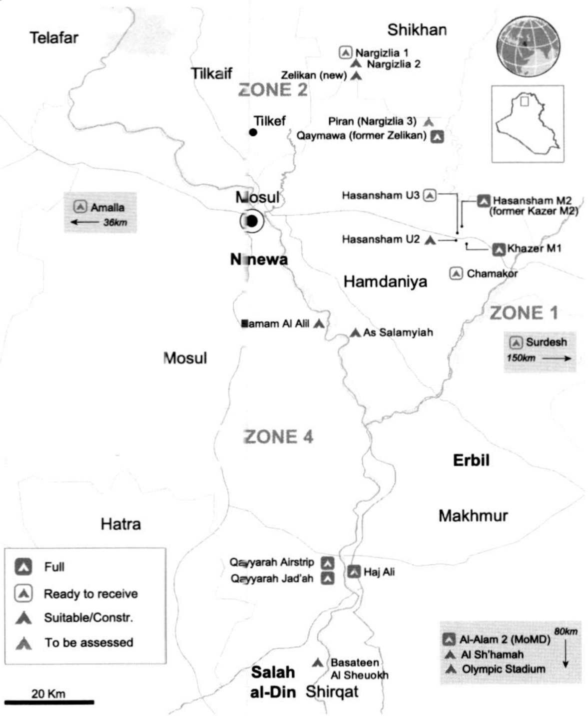

For planning purposes one plot = one family of 6 individuals. This relationship may vary depending on familiy size and preferences.
Creation date: 15 Jan 2017 **Sources:** OCHA, GoI, CCCM cluster, [1]IOM DTM, [1]Camp managers, [2]Not including another 26,000 plots planned by Ninewa Governorate. **Info:** johnston@unhcr.org

The boundaries and names shown and the designations used on this map do not imply official endorsement or acceptance by the United Nations.
The information reflected in this infographic is constantly changing and captures information available at the moment of production.

SOURCE: United Nations High Commission for Refugees in Erbil, Iraq.
RAND *RR2076-2.1*

camps administered by the KRG were not permitted freedom of movement as required by international norms; family separation was challenging to remedy; and camp workers feared for their safety.

When IDPs fled Mosul, they first crossed checkpoints staffed by the Iraqi Security Forces (ISF), the Popular Mobilization Forces (PMF) (an umbrella term for Iraq's state-sponsored local militias), or the peshmerga (KRG military forces). If the displaced men's names were not flagged in databases as members of ISIS, then they and their families were taken by bus to a camp. There was no international monitoring of the vetting process; monitoring officials from the International Committee for the Red Cross were present only in the official detention centers. Many temporary and informal screening centers were not being monitored, although USAID did deploy mobile protection and legal teams to attempt to fill some of the gaps.

After civilians were checked for weapons, vetted, and escorted to the camps, in some of the camps administered by the KRG, their identification documents were taken from them, and they were not allowed to move onward elsewhere in Iraq. UN and U.S. officials raised the lack of freedom of movement for the IDPs, a key humanitarian norm, as a particular concern about the camps. A senior UN official stated, "We have said to them that this is an acute problem. We continue to raise this. They confiscate the IDs. . . . This is completely unacceptable and we are continuing to press this."[16]

There were many cases of families being separated, according to UN, camp, and NGO officials.[17] Family separation could happen when family members left Mosul at different times, when a family member was detained for screening, or when a sick or injured person was sent elsewhere for treatment. Within the camps, mobile phones of IDPs were confiscated for security reasons, limiting the ability of family members to find each other. UN agencies and NGOs ran programs to support family reunification. They noted that it was particularly complicated to reunite families across internal Iraqi regional borders because of the government approvals required.

Furthermore, camp staff expressed fears that ISIS could undertake activities in the camp, intimidate the civilians, and make chaos.[18] One camp manager said that sometimes staff feared their lives were in danger, although the presence of security forces assuaged that. Camp staff also noted that there had been no significant problems to date, despite the concerns.

Camp Conditions

Problems with camp conditions include insufficiency in the number of spaces, the substandard quality of sites, and a lack of physical and mental health care.

---

[16] Telephone interview with UN official in Iraq, February 13, 2017.

[17] Interviews with UN, camp, and NGO officials, January 2017.

[18] Interview with IDP camp officials, Erbil, Iraq, January 2017.

Through February 2017, there were 13 emergency sites, with 7 more under construction, as shown in Figure 2.1. Through the operation for East Mosul, the number of spaces in camps had been sufficient because fewer people had been displaced than anticipated. UN and U.S. officials warned of future space shortages, should there be a large wave of IDPs from the operations in West Mosul.[19] As of March 2017, news reports described camp space shortages, with camps overflowing and thousands sleeping on the ground outside camps.[20] Both UN and U.S. officials said that the biggest barrier was availability of land, not financial resources; approvals for land use from the Iraqi government and KRG had been slow in coming.

The camps established for IDPs fleeing the battle of Mosul do not meet the Sphere standards, international standards for camps.[21] UN and U.S. officials noted that these were termed "emergency sites" and not camps for this reason.[22] The emergency site concept was employed because of the delay in land approvals; there was a rush to create bed space in tents, even if camps were not up to standards. The euphemistically termed emergency sites included plastic tents and lacked electricity, places to cook hot food, and tent space. UN officials said that the emergency sites could be upgraded if IDPs remained in camps longer than planned. Figure 2.2 shows a picture of Khazer I camp.

Health services in the camps were not comprehensive, with doctors available only during daytime hours, not at night. Camp staff used their private cars to transport people to hospitals; one displaced woman gave birth in a staff member's private car. NGO workers in one camp identified skin illnesses as a big issue in camps among "most children."[23] Lack of treatment for mental health was also a large gap, as many of the IDPs were traumatized. Furthermore, there was little to do in the camps to help the traumatized IDPs pass the time.

Challenges Returning Home

The intention of the Iraqi government was that IDPs would remain in the camps for a maximum of three months, until they could leave and return to their newly liberated homes. Yet, there were warning signs that the camp approach would not be sufficient; the policy placed people in temporary camps that were not up to the standards of longer-term camps for a situation that could last, with restricted freedom of movement

---

[19] Interview with U.S. officials in Washington, D.C., December 13, 2016; interviews with UN and U.S. officials, Erbil, Iraq, January 2017.

[20] Igor Kossov, "Mosul's Growing Humanitarian Crisis as Bad as Feared," *USA Today*, March 15, 2017. As of March 24, 2017: http://www.usatoday.com/story/news/world/2017/03/15/mosul-refugees-iraq-camps/99137150/.

[21] Sphere Project, "The Sphere Handbook." As of March 24, 2017: http://www.spherehandbook.org/.

[22] Interview with U.S. officials in Washington, D.C., December 13, 2016; interviews with UN officials, Erbil, Iraq, January 2017.

[23] Interview with IDP camp official, Erbil, Iraq, January 2017.

Figure 2.2
Families in Tents at Khazer I Camp

RAND *RR2076-2.2*

in some cases. Numerous officials recognized that returns were "not likely to be that rapid."[24] Given the lack of freedom of movement, some camps run the risk of turning into de facto detention camps.

UN officials expressed concern about trends they saw of delayed return permissions for some Arab communities from areas of Ninewa Province that are under de facto KRG and peshmerga control.[25] They were concerned that permissions from the KRG for Arab communities to return to these contested areas might not be forthcoming (as there was a perception that the KRG may aim to make these areas more ethnically Kurdish instead of Arab), putting in question the future of these communities.

---

24 Interviews with U.S. officials, Erbil, Iraq, January 2017; telephone interview with U.S. official in Erbil, Iraq, February 8, 2017.

25 Interviews with UN and U.S. officials, Erbil, Iraq, January 2017; telephone interview with UN official in Iraq, February 13, 2017.

Camp leadership also identified the problem of not having a clear process for people who want to go home.

Many IDPs fled without documentation. Of IDPs in the camps, 44 percent were missing at least one document, such as a birth certificate, marriage certificate, registration document, or ID.[26] This happened for several reasons: people fled without IDs, IDs were lost in transit because ISIS took them as fines,[27] and many marriages and births were not registered under ISIS. IDs are linked to basic citizenship rights, access to services and food assistance, and reunification of families. NGOs operated programs to assist IDPs with legal support for recovering documentation.

Some IDPs stayed in camps due to an inability to meet basic needs in liberated areas. UN and camp officials noted that they saw "fluidity" in the camps, with people leaving the camps only to return to them because of insufficient conditions at home.[28] If public services and markets had not returned to neighborhoods or villages, people found that they had better access to these in the camps. According to an IOM survey, the top five needs for returnees in other parts of liberated Iraq were drinking water, food, health care, income, and shelter.[29]

Circumstances of the IDPs from 2014–2015

The Situation

The 1.3 million IDPs from Ninewa who fled their homes before the battle moved elsewhere: other locations in Ninewa (438,000), Dohuk (382,000), and Erbil (146,000), with the remainder in smaller numbers in other provinces.[30] Across Iraq, 80 percent of IDPs were living in urban and other noncamp areas, with the remaining 20 percent in camps.[31] IDPs in urban areas lived with host families, in rented housing, in unfinished buildings, and in schools.[32] A camp official related that families were struggling in the urban areas and that there were waiting lists to move into the camps.[33]

---

26 UN Refugee Agency, 2017.

27 Interviews with UN and IDP camp officials, Erbil, Iraq, January 2017.

28 Interviews with UN and IDP camp officials, Erbil, Iraq, January 2017.

29 IOM: Iraq Mission, "Returnee Location Assessment Report," *ReliefWeb*, October 2016b. As of March 27, 2017: http://reliefweb.int/sites/reliefweb.int/files/resources/IOM%20DTM%20Returnee%20Location%20Assessment%20Report_October_2016.pdf.

30 IOM: Iraq Mission, 2017a.

31 IOM: Iraq Mission, 2017a.

32 IOM: Iraq Mission, 2017a.

33 Interview with IDP camp official, Erbil, Iraq, January 2017.

The Response and Needs

Assistance to these IDPs was provided by the Iraqi central and provincial governments, UN agencies, implementing NGO partners, and local religious communities.

The first consideration for this group was dwindling assistance and attention. A U.S. official noted that although circumstances for this group of Mosul IDPs were "relatively stable," both humanitarian and government assistance had shifted away, toward the newly displaced. Assistance was no longer for all IDPs but rather targeted the most vulnerable.[34] One camp official mentioned shrinking amounts of food assistance in particular.[35] Indeed, because of a lack of donor funding, the WFP halved its food rations to the 1.4 million Iraqi IDPs it was supporting in January 2017.[36] U.S. and camp officials said that church groups in the Kurdistan Region, drawing on private and international funds, were the only entities providing rent assistance to some IDPs (the Christians).[37]

These IDPs experienced high rates of poverty, high unemployment, and low access to education. Because of the ongoing financial crisis in Iraq, many IDPs had trouble finding work; humanitarian assistance was insufficient to fully meet their needs.[38] A mitigating factor was that government employees from Mosul and other parts of Ninewa Province still received their government salaries. Across Iraq, 70 percent of displaced children had missed an entire year of school.[39] Only about 45 percent of displaced children in camps and 30 percent out of camps were in school, setting this generation up for serious challenges in completing education, contributing to the workforce, and finding family-sustaining jobs.[40]

The large numbers of IDPs living in nearby cities, towns, and villages placed strains on host community public services (such as health care, education, water and sanitation, and electricity), as well as on markets for housing and jobs. For example, nearby Erbil experienced a 30 percent increase in population since 2014 due to the 1.8 million displaced people that they hosted (Syrian refugees and Iraqi IDPs from Ninewa and other parts of Iraq). They offered public services such as education and health care

---

34 Telephone interview with U.S. official in Erbil, Iraq, February 8, 2017.

35 Interview with IDP camp official, Erbil, Iraq, January 2017.

36 "UN Agency Cuts Food Aid to 1.4 Million Displaced Iraqis," *Al Jazeera*, January 28, 2017. As of March 28, 2017: http://www.aljazeera.com/news/2017/01/food-aid-displaced-iraqis-170128051248193.html.

37 Interview with U.S. official and IDP camp officials, Erbil, Iraq, January 2017.

38 Erbil Refugee Council, UNHCR, Erbil Statistics Directorate, Joint Crisis Coordination Centre, IOM, United Nations Population Fund, UN-Habitat, and UNOCHA, *Displacement as Challenge and Opportunity, Urban Profile of Refugees, Internally Displaced Persons and Host Community: Erbil Governorate, Kurdistan Region of Iraq*, May 2016. As of March 28, 2017: http://reliefweb.int/sites/reliefweb.int/files/resources/ErbilUrbanProfilingApril2016English.pdf.

39 UNICEF, "Reaching Children in Iraq," February 10, 2017b. As of March 24, 2017: https://www.unicef.org/infobycountry/iraq_74784.html.

40 UNOCHA, *Iraq Humanitarian Response Plan*, June 2015. As of March 24, 2017: http://reliefweb.int/sites/reliefweb.int/files/resources/2015-Iraq-Humanitarian-Response-Plan%20%281%29.pdf.

to the IDPs, but the ongoing financial crisis precluded concomitant additional funding for the increased demands on public services.[41] The KRG estimated that they spent $120 million per month on refugee and IDP-related expenses.[42]

The 2014–2015 IDPs could be more hesitant to return to their homes than those displaced by the military offensive to retake Mosul. Officials interviewed believed that the number of returns among this community was low, based on interactions with representatives of the displaced communities.[43] Members of many communities did not wish to return to their original homes for several reasons. Minority communities that had been targeted by ISIS and fled (such as the Yazidis, Christians, Turkman, and Shabaks) remained concerned about their security if they returned; they viewed neighboring communities as complicit in the atrocities against them and did not trust the government to provide protection. Many had little to return to, as ISIS destroyed homes, public buildings, places of worship, and businesses in many communities and left other communities heavily mined. The director of a settlement of displaced Christians in Erbil stated that few, if any, of these Iraqis wanted to return home.[44] A former resident of Mosul, he recounted threats he personally received, and he noted that such pressures against Christians in Ninewa had been present for many years. After several years away, many had begun establishing new lives by reestablishing communities, jobs, and education elsewhere, providing further incentive to stay in their new locations. The Christians and Yazidis in particular were successful at obtaining visas in Western countries. Because of these considerations, it will be necessary to have different strategies for those displaced by ISIS in 2014–2015 and those IDPs displaced by the military operations.

Conclusion

The population of Ninewa Province has undergone a number of traumas: being conquered by ISIS, living through military operations, living under ISIS, being displaced, living in camps, integrating into new Iraqi cities, losing home and community, and facing prospects of difficulty in returning to their homes because of destroyed property or conflicts with neighboring communities. Circumstances have varied among Moslawis in different circumstances: those living inside Mosul, who have experienced life under ISIS and military operations to retake the city; those who have fled the military operations to live mainly in emergency sites that were set up with the intention of being

---

41 Kurdistan Region of Iraq Erbil Governorate, *Displacement as Challenge and Opportunity, Erbil Profile*, April 2016.

42 Interview with senior KRG official, Erbil, Iraq, January 2017.

43 Telephone interview with U.S. official in Erbil, Iraq, February 8, 2017.

44 Interview with IDP camp official, Erbil, Iraq, January 2017.

temporary; and those who fled ISIS in 2014 and 2015 to live in urban settings or camps elsewhere in Iraq. These people face disparate challenges in their current settings; displaced people face varied barriers to their prospects for returning home. Managing their current humanitarian and protection needs, as well as the process of IDP returns, will require careful planning and implementation.

While this chapter has focused on the humanitarian needs and displacement of people from Mosul, the issues here also echo particularly the displacement issues faced by people in other provinces affected by ISIS. Solutions for Iraq's 3 million displaced people must come from both local and national levels. At the national level, resources, policies, decisions, and coordination will be required, as well as the coordination of returns of IDPs when they cross Iraqi provincial borders.

CHAPTER THREE

Postcombat Security Conditions

This chapter reviews the combat operations against ISIS in Mosul and the surrounding areas of Ninewa Province, then describes and assesses three near-term challenges for establishing a safe and secure environment as part of the humanitarian assistance and stabilization effort. The provision of security is a bedrock element required for stabilizing the country and enabling displaced civilians to return home. Although numerous security challenges affect the prospects for stabilization, stakeholder interviews and other research for this project suggest that the three urgent requirements for postcombat security are the following: (1) expanded demining to address the widespread incidence of ERW, which mostly consist of the improvised explosive devices (IEDs) that ISIS uses extensively in both offensive and defensive warfare; (2) adequate, competent hold forces that remain in liberated areas immediately after offensive combat operations; and (3) the generation and deployment of quality police forces that will assume the local security role.

Other issues also impact the security environment in Mosul and the other conflict-affected areas of Iraq, including the long-term plan for developing security forces and the eventual disposition of militia groups under the PMF law approved in late 2016. Iraq will require competent security forces even after the major combat operations are finished, as ISIS remnants are likely to return to guerrilla mode and, in the worst case, could retake areas. The PMF law legalizes both Shia and Sunni mobilization forces that were formed as local militias but brought under state control; the language of the law is broad, however, and implementation regulations had not been issued as of May 2017. It is unclear whether the Sunni forces might eventually be transformed into provincial security forces, as foreseen in an earlier proposal issued by Iraq's prime minister. In addition, many of the Shia militia groups are controlled by powerful political figures, many of whom have close ties with Iran.[1] In Mosul, the Shia PMF was kept out of the city and therefore did not commit abuses or create the political problems that it had in Fallujah, other environs in Anbar, and Tikrit and elsewhere in Salah al-Din. The potential for the use of the Shia PMF causing problems in Sunni-majority areas

1 For more detailed discussion of these issues, see Linda Robinson, *Assessment of the Politico-Military Campaign to Counter ISIL and Options for Adaptation*, Santa Monica, Calif.: RAND Corporation, 2016.

remained high in future operations planned for western Ninewa, the Hawija area, and elsewhere.

While these long-term issues of overall security force capacity and the future of the PMF are important, RAND's analysis identified the three issues cited previously as urgent for both establishing security and technical prerequisites for making progress on the longer-term issues. As of May 2017, RAND's analysis concluded that these issues were insufficiently prioritized and funded to achieve the intended objectives.

The salience of these three issues is not limited to Mosul and the surrounding Ninewa Province; the same issues pertain to all five conflict-affected provinces. In addition, these are national-level issues because providing adequate security in these areas of Iraq depends on national-level planning, decisionmaking, funding, and implementation. Resources devoted to demining, as well as to the development and deployment of both hold forces and permanent police forces, also fall under the purview of the Baghdad government, and they are heavily influenced by support provided by the Coalition.

The Combat Phase

The battle for Mosul proceeded in three phases. After a months-long buildup and progressive operations to retake outlying villages and isolate Mosul, combat operations commenced on October 17, 2016, in East Mosul (also known in Iraq as the Left Bank). Iraqi forces attacked along three axes: from the north, from east to west on a central axis, and from the south. The KRG peshmerga forces conducted operations to clear ISIS forces from the eastern Ninewa plains, and Federal Police forces, including its Emergency Response Division, followed the main body of Iraqi army units to secure areas cleared of ISIS.

The first phase of the offensive operations bogged down due to fierce counterattacks and heavy fighting, as well as the Iraqi forces' uncoordinated movements along the three axes. Following an operational pause in December, Iraqi security leaders conferred and adopted a more synchronized approach. Coalition military advisers reinforced conventional units and aided the Iraqi Counter Terrorism Service in executing a dramatic nighttime operation that cleared a path to the east bank of the Tigris River, cutting ISIS forces in half. The Coalition blocked ISIS reinforcements from West Mosul by bombing the bridges and conducting strikes against fighters attempting to cross the river by boat. This second phase ended in late January with the declaration by the Baghdad government that East Mosul had been secured. Another pause ensued for units to regroup, tend to the extensive casualties, refit with ammunition, and replace numerous damaged armored vehicles. The third phase, the offensive against ISIS fighters holding the remaining city areas of West Mosul, commenced on February 20, 2017.

The operations to seize West Mosul progressed more rapidly than expected in the first weeks, but the pace slowed as Iraq's security forces reached the densely populated, narrow streets of the Old City area of West Mosul. ISIS waged a counterattack to wrest back control of the government center complex, just south of the Old City.

Throughout the Mosul campaign, the Iraqi forces limited the use of artillery and air strikes in order to observe Prime Minister Haider al-Abadi's overarching order that civilian casualties be avoided to the maximum extent possible. Iraqi army spokesman BG Tahseen Ibrahim said of the 500 Iraqi soldiers killed and approximately 3,000 wounded in East Mosul[2] to one of the authors in a February meeting, "We took casualties ourselves in order to spare the civilians."[3] The security forces largely avoided indiscriminate use of artillery in many battles, relying instead on direct fire by maneuver units, but civilian casualties and physical destruction did occur. Some 1,283 civilians are estimated to have died and another 969 are estimated to have been wounded in the operations for East Mosul and the Ninewa plains between October 2016 and January 2017, according to UN statistics.[4]

Civilian casualties increased notably as the West Mosul operations reached the densely populated Old City quarter. Airwars, a nonprofit group that monitors strikes, said the casualties had more than doubled by its count, and on March 17, a coalition air strike in the al-Jadida district struck a building, killing at least 112 civilians and possibly up to 200. U.S. Central Command initiated an investigation into the strike, and eyewitnesses reported that fighters were on the rooftop while families were huddled in the basement of the building.[5] USCENTCOM reaffirmed that its procedures sought to avoid civilian casualties, despite press speculation that the Trump administration had relaxed the standards for air strikes. LTG Steve Townsend, the U.S. coalition commander, stated that procedures allowed for more rapid approval of air strikes than had

2 Gordon, 2017a.

3 Interview with BG Ibrahim, Baghdad, February 22, 2017.

4 United Nations Iraq, "UN Casualty Figures for Iraq for the Month of October 2016," November 1, 2016a. As of March 27, 2017: http://www.uniraq.org/index.php?option=com_k2&view=item&id=6267:un-casualty-figures-for-iraq-for-the-month-of-october-2016&Itemid=633&lang=en; United Nations Iraq, "UN Casualty Figures for Iraq for the Month of November 2016," December 2, 2016c. As of March 27, 2017: http://www.uniraq.org/index.php?option=com_k2&view=item&id=6455:un-casualty-figures-for-iraq-for-the-month-of-november-2016&Itemid=633&lang=en; United Nations Iraq, "UN Casualties Figures for Iraq for the Month of December 2016," January 3, 2017a. As of March 27, 2017: http://www.uniraq.org/index.php?option=com_k2&view=item&id=6611:un-casualties-figures-for-iraq-for-the-month-of-december-2016&Itemid=633&lang=en; United Nations Iraq, "UN Casualties Figures for Iraq for the Month of January 2017," February 2, 2017b. As of March 27, 2017: http://www.uniraq.org/index.php?option=com_k2&view=item&id=6725:un-casualties-figures-for-iraq-for-the-month-of-january-2017&Itemid=633&lang=en.

5 Tim Arango and Helene Cooper, "U.S. Investigating Mosul Strikes Said to Have Killed Up to 200 Civilians," *New York Times*, March 29, 2017.

occurred under the Obama administration, but that the requirement to avoid civilian casualties remained in place.[6]

As the fight continued, civilians began to flow out of West Mosul at rates exceeding 10,000 a day. The Iraqi forces adapted their approach to allow civilians trapped in the Old City to escape between the multiple prongs of their attack, but ISIS snipers gunned down fleeing civilians and held others as human shields. The combat phase appeared to be ending as summer approached, turning attention to the follow-on operations elsewhere and the need to stabilize a traumatized city.

Explosive Hazards

The prevalence of mines, booby-traps, IEDs, unexploded ordnance, and other ERW is one of the biggest near-term and long-term challenges to the stabilization of Mosul and other parts of Ninewa Province. While surveys of the extent of explosive hazards were incomplete, there are indications that the number of devices left by ISIS is large and their reach widespread. Explosive hazards cause deaths and injuries and prohibit people from returning to their homes, potentially for years. The current explosive hazard mitigation efforts are focused on public infrastructure and particular geographic areas; U.S. and international officials acknowledged that currently funded programs do not address those left in homes, workplaces, or agricultural fields.

The Extent of the Problem

This section's analysis relies heavily on the evidence of mines and efforts at demining in liberated parts of Ninewa Province and other areas of Iraq, since the ongoing combat operations prevented surveys on the exact magnitude of explosive hazards in Mosul itself. While the ERW extent was still unknown in Mosul, indications from other liberated Iraqi cities, other towns and villages in Ninewa Province, and early reports from Mosul indicated levels would be formidable. Officials described the levels of contamination as "massive."[7] ISIS often left IEDs, not traditional ordnance, such as those made with pressure pots and pipes.

Ninewa had some very contaminated areas. Conditions in some liberated towns and villages were not safe enough to allow civilians to return to their homes. Sinjar, a Yazidi town in Ninewa, had such extensive IED contamination that the UNDP

6 Michael R. Gordon, "U.S. 'Probably Had a Role' in Mosul Deaths, Commander Says," *New York Times*, March 28, 2017b.

7 Interview with U.S. official in Iraq, January 31, 2017; interview with U.S. officials in Washington, D.C., December 13, 2016; interview with NGO official, Erbil, Iraq, January 2017; telephone interview with NGO official in Erbil, Iraq, March 1, 2017.

stopped all work until it could be assessed.[8] One Shabak village of 22 families had 200 mines, according to data provided by the KRG. In the village of Tulaband, formerly occupied by ISIS and southeast of Mosul, there were 551 landmines in a village of previously 450 families, according to data provided by the Mine Action Group. The water treatment plant in the Ninewa town of Bartallah was so heavily mined that it would need to be detonated rather than cleared. There were indications that villages with people in them were not as contaminated as empty villages, but these villages could have defensive lines of mines. Figure 3.1 illustrates the extent of known ERW hazards in Mosul, Ninewa Province, and elsewhere in northern Iraq as of March 2017, before the military operations were complete. New hazards, and even some hazards predating ISIS, are as yet unknown, as surveys have not been completed.

Early assessments already found heavy explosive contamination in Mosul.[9] Key liberated areas were mined—for example, the airport and south of the city. Expectations were that East Mosul was heavily mined, but not as bad as Ramadi, which ISIS had heavily mined after civilians fled (see Box 3.1). Circumstances in West Mosul were unknown, but U.S. and UN officials expected that West Mosul could be as bad as Ramadi. As Mosul was ISIS's last major stand, one U.S. official anticipated West Mosul to have "the nastiest explosive threats that they have employed anywhere."[10] A potentially mitigating factor was that people had continued living in Mosul rather than abandoning the city, somewhat reducing the ability of insurgents to place mines.

The problem of explosive hazards extends beyond those planted by ISIS. Areas of Ninewa Province are still mined from the previous Gulf wars. Extensive minefields also remain along the perimeters of the Kurdistan Region and along borders with Iran, Turkey, and Syria. One demining official described it as "one of the most heavily contaminated sites in the world before ISIS."[11] In 2004, the Iraqi government conducted a landmine impact survey; in the years since then, the government, humanitarian NGOs, and private oil companies have worked to demine some areas. Even so, they are "just scratching the surface," as described by the demining official.

Consequences

The presence of such a large number of explosive hazards has significant consequences. First is the likelihood of high casualties. Per Figure 3.1, there were 2,470 security incidents involving explosive hazards in northern Iraq from 2014 through March 2017. For example, in 2016, the governor of Anbar called for civilians to return to Ramadi

---

8 UNDP in Iraq, *Funding Facility for Immediate Stabilization: Quarterly Progress Report, Q3—Year 2016*, 2016a.

9 UNOCHA, "Iraq: Mosul Humanitarian Response Situation Report #7 (7–13 November 2016) [En/Ar/Ku]," *ReliefWeb*, November 14, 2016b. As of March 24, 2017: http://reliefweb.int/report/iraq/iraq-mosul-humanitarian-response-situation-report-7-7-13-november-2016-enarku.

10 Interview with U.S official in Iraq, January 31, 2017.

11 Interview with NGO official, Erbil, Iraq, January 2017.

Figure 3.1
Explosive Hazards in Northern Iraq

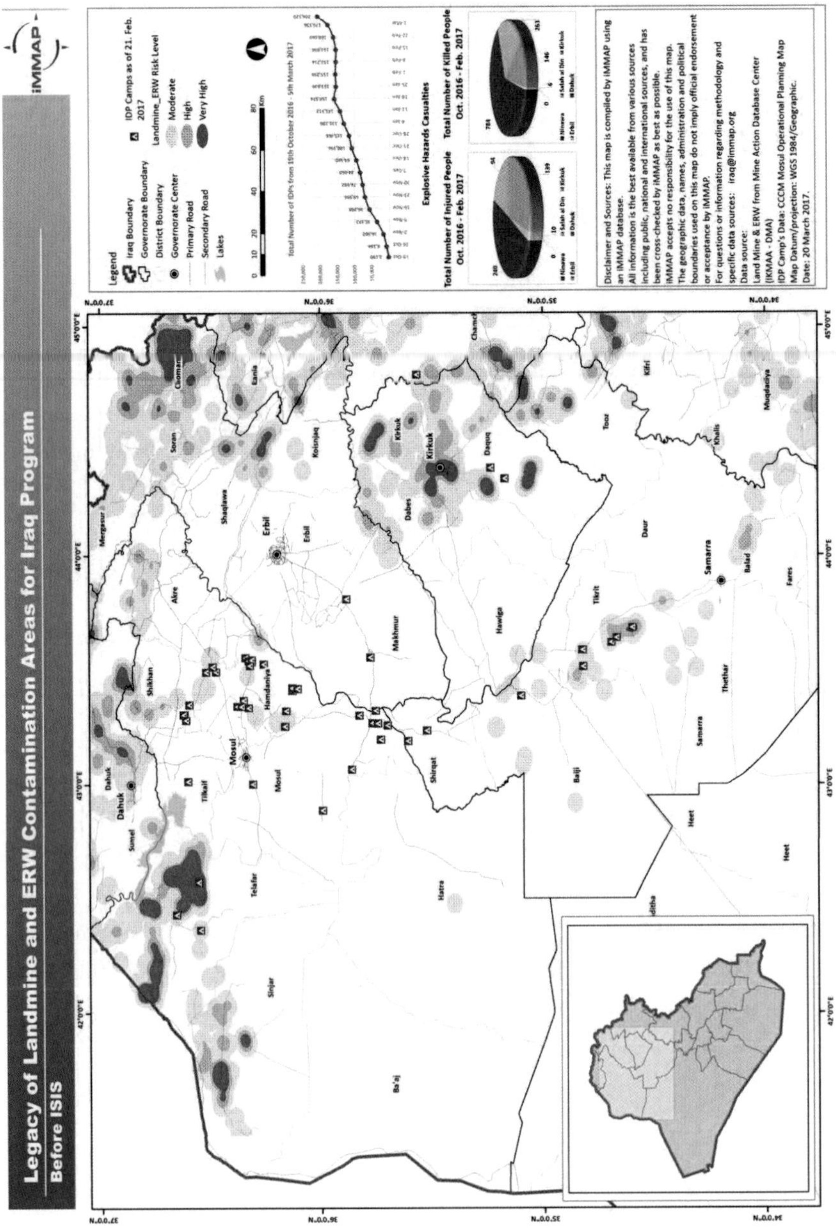

SOURCES: Data and graphic provided to authors by iMMap, Iraq, for the purpose of this report.
RAND *RR2076-3.1*

Box 3.1 Explosive Hazards in Other Liberated Cities

A main issue preventing or delaying IDP returns to other liberated cities was ERW contamination. This was particularly the case for Ramadi and Fallujah, and to a lesser extent Tikrit. Ramadi was one of the "most explosive contaminated places on earth," according to a U.S. official;[12] ISIS created layers of defensive bombs in key terrain in the city. In Ramadi, Fallujah and Karma, more than 1,800 explosive hazards were cleared in the latter half of 2016 by the FFIS at 188 priority sites.[13] ISIS booby-trapped houses of people who opposed them, such as government officials. They laid IEDs in places without defensive value, such as in front of pharmacies, schools and clinics, where people were likely to return. U.S. officials interviewed estimated that demining activity would be required for years or even decades in Ramadi.[14] Janus, a demining firm hired by the State Department, had cleared 600,000 square km in Anbar and Salah al-Din Provinces, finding 25,000 KG of explosive ordnance (IEDs, grenades, ammunition, and mines).[15] The total would likely rise as clearance activities continued.

RAND *RR2076-box3.1*

before the city was cleared; 200 civilians died from IEDs.[16] Second, explosive hazards inhibit IDPs from returning home or force them to leave once they have returned, moving back to camps or onward to other cities. Third, explosive hazards make areas inaccessible for the provision of humanitarian assistance, the provision of public services, or the rebuilding of infrastructure. And fourth, heavy mining of the homes of minorities and those who disagreed with ISIS makes their returns even more challenging. For example, in Ramadi, ISIS did not booby-trap homes of ISIS sympathizers, according to a U.S. official.[17] That meant that the families that could return home the quickest were often those of the insurgents. The pace of returns and stabilization activities will depend significantly on the pace of explosive hazard removal.

Activities to Address Explosive Hazard Mitigation

Iraq had taken a novel approach to explosive hazard mitigation in an effort to get civilians back home more quickly. Rather than wait until areas were fully secure, in Tikrit,

---

12 Interview with U.S. official in Iraq, January 31, 2017.

13 UN Assistance Mission for Iraq, "Briefing to the Security Council by Srsg for Iraq Ján Kubiš; New York, 9 November 2016 [En/Ar]," *ReliefWeb*, November 9, 2016. As of March 24, 2017: http://reliefweb.int/report/iraq/briefing-security-council-srsg-iraq-j-n-kubi-new-york-9-november-2016-enar.

14 Interview with U.S. officials, Baghdad, February 22, 2017.

15 Data provided by U.S. Department of State to authors.

16 Stephen Kalin, "Iraqi Military Freezes Civilians' Return to Ramadi over Mine Deaths," Reuters, April 24, 2016. As of March 24, 2017: http://www.reuters.com/article/us-mideast-crisis-iraq-ramadi-idUSKCN0XL0OL.

17 Interview with U.S. officials in Washington, D.C., December 13, 2016.

Ramadi, and Fallujah, demining contractors moved in directly behind the hold forces that arrived to secure areas after the initial combat phase. These efforts were focused on clearing key infrastructure to enable public services to resume: water and power lines and sewage plants were first, followed by schools and health clinics. Specific locations were decided by the Iraqi government in consultation with the UN. This focused and rapid demining effort aimed to enable roads to open and essential services to restart.

However, the current programs for explosive hazard mitigation are insufficient to fully handle the problem, given its magnitude. Many important areas remained laced with mines. No comprehensive plan exists to clear urban spaces, residences, or agricultural areas. One Iraqi general stated to us, "The Iraqi military doesn't have capability to find all mines and explosive materials."[18] While the Coalition provided counter-IED training and equipment to the Iraqi Security Forces, their efforts were focused on clearing mines to facilitate the combat operations, not on mine clearing in the stabilization phase that follows. A KRG official said, "It is beyond our capacity. We need help."[19] A U.S. official noted, "Even with ten times the current resources of now, we couldn't demine the country."[20]

The private-sector company Janus was the largest demining effort (with $41 million from April 2016 until spent, with likely more available afterward), about two-thirds funded by the U.S. State Department. Janus had 100 people working in Ramadi and was training teams for Ninewa. There were plans to move demining efforts into East Mosul once hold forces were situated. The United Nations Mine Action Service (UNMAS) also funded and managed humanitarian demining, relying on bilateral contributions to the UN Voluntary Trust Fund for Assistance in Mine Action; they requested $112 million in 2016. At the end of 2016, this demining request was mostly unfunded.[21] UNMAS subcontracted with the private-sector company Optima. The demining forces were Iraqis, trained by the private companies in a monthlong course. Janus and Optima conducted this focused demining effort in Ramadi and Fallujah, before moving on to Mosul.

The Iraqi government, led by the Directorate of Mine Action in Baghdad and the Iraqi Kurdish Mine Authority, and private companies hired by the oil and gas industry had conducted legacy demining. The peshmerga also conducted demining, yet officials we interviewed viewed the peshmerga as lacking capacity according to international standards, taking large casualties because of this.[22] Iraq's financial crisis hobbled the Iraqi government's ability to fund demining.

---

18 Interview with Iraqi military official in Erbil, Iraq, January 2017.

19 Interview with senior KRG official, Erbil, Iraq, January 2017.

20 Interview with U.S. official in Iraq, January 31, 2017; telephone interview with U.S. official in Iraq, February 1, 2017.

21 UN Assistance Mission for Iraq, 2016.

22 Interview with NGO official, Erbil, Iraq, January 2017.

In addition, NGOs were conducting demining efforts in areas outside major combat operations, such as Kirkuk and the Ninewa plains. Fifteen humanitarian demining NGOs operated in northern Iraq. NGO capacity was limited. The Mine Action Group was the biggest demining NGO operating in Iraq, with seven teams. To give an idea of the scope of the problem, it took the Mine Action Group five months with all its teams to clear one heavily mined village (Tulaband), at the cost of $600,000.

Demining is expensive and risky, even with trained staff. Different entities have different levels of risk tolerance. Some areas were still so risky because of security threats that even if there were large demining tenders, it would be difficult to get bidders, according to both U.S. officials and NGOs.[23] The security environment was such that deminers faced risks from snipers, car bombs, and more. This set this situation apart from traditional humanitarian demining. U.S. officials noted that hiring private companies (Janus and Optima) to do humanitarian demining was a new and controversial paradigm; traditionally, aid agencies prefer to work with NGOs for humanitarian demining instead of private companies.[24] However, NGOs lack both the capacity and the risk tolerance to address these risks at this scale.

Water, power, and sewage were prioritized for demining, followed by schools, clinics, main commercial streets, and public buildings, according to officials interviewed.[25] None of the stabilization demining efforts were demining housing because resources were inadequate. Demining housing posed a political risk, one U.S. official noted, requiring decisions to demine the homes of some people before others, which may be perceived as preferential treatment for one group over another.[26] Similarly, demining efforts were not conducted or planned for areas between villages. Officials disagreed about priorities, noting that if a village were cleared but not its agricultural fields, returning villagers would not be able to support themselves or would face risks doing so.[27]

In addition to the actual work of demining, preliminary surveys and threat assessments are required to map the scope of the problem and prioritize areas. Public safety education programs and capacity building are other essential components of an orchestrated approach. A number of related activities were under way. Surveys were being conducted through the FFIS, involving UNMAS and subcontractors. iMMAP, an international humanitarian organization that provides information management in emergencies, managed databases from Iraqi government, KRG, and publicly available information sources to provide mapping of ERW. Next, NGOs (with funding from

---

[23] Interview with U.S. official in Iraq, January 31, 2017; interview with NGO official, Erbil, Iraq, January 2017.

[24] Interview with NGO official, Erbil, Iraq, January 2017; telephone interview with U.S. official in Iraq, February 1, 2017.

[25] Interview with UN official, Erbil, Iraq, January 2017.

[26] Interview with U.S. official in Iraq, January 31, 2017.

[27] Interview with NGO official, Erbil, Iraq, January 2017.

the United States and other donors) conducted risk education for civilians so that they could recognize and avoid explosive risks. The next activity was building Iraqi capacity for demining, as demining was not something that a small number of expert expatriates in Iraq could fully accomplish. For example, Janus, the Mine Action Group, and others hired local Iraqis who were connected to their communities. This also provided local employment. Capacity building would be needed for police and security forces. "I can't think of a better use of U.S. taxpayer funds" in Iraq, said one U.S. official.[28] Finally, the Iraqi Ministry of Displacement and Migration and the KRG Joint Communication Center signed an agreement to develop a joint plan to assess mine contamination and communicate when it is safe to return home; so far they have not developed this strategy. Given the magnitude of the problem, greater progress on this critical issue would likely require a combined approach that involves more funding for wider demining, as well as expanded efforts to map hazards, create Iraqi demining capability, and educate the public.

Temporary Hold Forces After Mosul Clearing Operations

The immediate plan for securing Mosul after major combat operations against ISIS, designed collaboratively by the Iraqi government and the Coalition, called for a portion of those combat forces to remain in place to secure the city in order to augment the still-nascent police forces and the tribal forces that had been trained and fielded to perform security functions. The numbers required for hold or stability operations were based, among other sources, on RAND research establishing a ratio of 20 troops per 1,000 people.[29] The estimated 450,000 population of East Mosul and the estimated 750,000 population of West Mosul, totaling 1.2 million, would require a hold force of 60,000 troops.

The East Mosul hold force consisted of troops from the 16th Iraqi Army Division, the Federal Police, and the nascent police forces. In addition, a collection of tribal and minority forces from Ninewa were trained and employed, largely under the umbrella of the Iraqi government's PMF. Some additional Ninewa local forces have been trained by the KRG Zerevani special police force, paramilitary police who have been trained by Coalition partners.

A major stabilizing role was being played by the KRG peshmerga forces in a large swath of Ninewa Province to the east of Mosul called the Ninewa plains. The peshmerga had effectively become the hold force for all the terrain they had secured since

---

28 Telephone interview with U.S. official in Iraq, February 1, 2017.

29 James T. Quinlivan, "Force Requirements in Stability Operations," *Parameters*, Vol. 25, No. 4, 1995, pp. 59–60; James T. Quinlivan, "Burden of Victory: The Painful Arithmetic of Stability Operations," *RAND Review*, Vol. 27, No. 2, Summer 2003, p. 200.

the inception of the counter-ISIS campaign in August 2014. Strictly controlled checkpoints and a defensive berm pointed to the quasi-permanent nature of their presence, and several officials stated that the Baghdadi government has tacitly agreed to this role. The Iraqi Security Forces would be hard-pressed to provide hold forces for the entire Ninewa Province, especially given that additional fighting was expected as ISIS reverted to counterinsurgency and used remaining sanctuaries in the Euphrates River Valley and Hawija to mount counterattacks.

Although East Mosul experienced some counterattacks by ISIS during the spring, the hold force appeared to be maintaining a reasonable level of security. Despite the patchwork of forces and the largely Shia composition of the army and federal police forces, the formula appeared to be working, at least in the short term. Few allegations of abuse by security forces were reported during the major operations in East Mosul.[30] A Baghdad official stated that many Moslawis were using a government hotline to provide tips on ISIS fighters' whereabouts.[31] "The citizens of Mosul have decided to reject Daesh," he said. "The Moslawis have changed their attitudes since 2014." Numerous interviewees also noted that the absence of the Shia PMF inside Mosul proper constituted another hopeful development, as these forces committed abuses in Diyala, Fallujah, and elsewhere; however, concerns persisted about their presence on the outskirts of Mosul and in the western Tal Afar region of Ninewa.

Other interviewees expressed concerns about possible problems ahead, including reprisals and the looting of vacant homes.[32] Returnees in other cities faced problems including physical danger, legal entanglements with local authorities, threats and recruitment from armed groups, targeted violence on the basis of ethno-religious affiliation, and kidnapping.[33]

The tribal hold forces formally belonged to the Iraqi PMF, which originated after ISIS surged into Iraqi cities in 2014. The Grand Ayatollah Ali al-Sistani, based in Iraq's southern city of Najaf and widely considered the most senior religious leader among all Shia Muslim clerics, called on Iraqis to take up arms to defend the country, and large numbers of Shia responded. In addition, long-standing Shia militias with strong ties to Iran launched into action. Many of those militia leaders have been involved in the PMF leadership. In December 2016 the Iraqi parliament, the Council of Representatives, passed a law making the PMF a permanent element of Iraq's security forces; it reports directly to the prime minister through the Iraqi National Security Service, which is roughly equivalent to the U.S. National Security Council.

---

30 Martin Chulov, "Iraqi Forces Seize Mosul Airport from Isis as Syrian Rebels Take Al-Bab," *Guardian*, February 24, 2017. As of March 24, 2017: https://www.theguardian.com/world/2017/feb/23/iraqi-forces-storm-mosul-airport-seize-isis.

31 Interview with Saeed Al Jaishy, Baghdad, February 22, 2017.

32 Interviews with U.S. officials in Washington, D.C., January 2017, and Baghdad, February 22, 2017.

33 IOM: Iraq Mission, 2016b.

The Iraqi government authorized Sunni forces to be inducted into the PMF as well. The Sunni tribal leaders nominated recruits, and the government approved their enrollment and authorized their payment. U.S. special operations forces and other Coalition forces provided them weeklong training, oversaw training by Iraqi forces, and issued individual soldiers weapons. According to Coalition military personnel interviewed by the research team, Sunni tribal forces did contribute to security operations in Anbar, primarily because the local Iraqi commander of the 7th army division employed them effectively in concert with the army. However, officials also acknowledged that the program had yielded fewer results in Ninewa. Even in Anbar, some interviewees viewed the program as a payoff to prevent the tribes from fighting the government, rather than as an actual security force.[34]

A total of 8,200 recruits from Ninewa were accepted by the Iraqi government, which set aside 15,840 slots for entrants from the province. The actual training and arming of these forces proceeded slowly, however. Statistics provided by officials connected to the tribal forces program showed that a total of only 1,268 had been trained by the Coalition as of January 2017. These forces were arrayed in 14 "battalions" under the sponsorship of 14 different tribal sheikhs or local notables, including Ninewa governor Nawful Hamadi Sultan. Another 900 forces were scheduled for training in January. The officials expressed skepticism about the numbers, saying that often those enrolled failed to show up for training or other individuals appeared in their place.

Another component of the Ninewa tribal forces is the Ninewa Guard of former Ninewa governor Atheel Nujaifi, whose forces were trained by Turkey. He agreed to bring his 2,500 guards under the PMF umbrella, and they have been deployed as part of the hold force. An Iraqi official stated that Nujaifi's force had been deployed on the perimeter of Mosul, not in the center, and had agreed to work with the 16th Division.

As this brief description illustrates, the tribal forces have political affiliations that could skew their image and behavior as impartial providers of security. Generally, these forces were considered most effective when employed in their local areas. As far as competence, most of them had received only a week or two of training, which was barely adequate to enable them to man checkpoints. The hold force program of instruction included training in the laws of armed conflict, small arms and individual tactical skills, awareness of explosive hazards, combat lifesaver skills, tactical site exploitation, checkpoint operations, squad tactics, and command and leadership.

The tribal force program was intended not only to play a role in securing areas taken over by ISIS but also to foster political reconciliation by demonstrating the Iraqi government's commitment to incorporating the Sunni minority into security forces and to empower it to perform roles in Sunni areas. However, the recently passed PMF law did not clearly enumerate how these forces will be preserved, constituted, and commanded in the future. In an interview, National Security Service spokesman Saeed

---

[34] Interviews with U.S. officials in Erbil, Iraq, January 2017, and Baghdad, February 2017.

al-Jaishy said that although the PMF was a permanent element of the Iraqi Security Forces, it would remain under Baghdad's command rather than devolve to provincial governors' command. "Ninewa security details will wait until the elections," he said, adding that there may be no need for the forces when ISIS is defeated.[35]

The language of the PMF law was vague, in any event, and further implementation of regulations or legislation would be required to clarify the future of the program. Without further clarification, the tribal forces effort was not likely to assuage Sunni concerns and desires for security forces they trusted. In addition, if the PMF remained a permanent and separate force, frictions and competition with the other three forces—the army, the federal police, and the special operations Counter-Terrorism Service—for resources and recruits would be likely.

Creating a Sustainable Police Force

Development of a competent, professional police force is an essential ingredient for long-term security and the success of the counter-ISIS campaign. Iraq suffered from a lack of sufficient, well-trained police forces, and from the politicization of the Ministry of Interior, which had been largely staffed by the Shia members of the Badr Organization. In addition, many local police forces experienced high desertion rates as ISIS took over territory in 2013–2014; thousands of Iraqi soldiers and police were executed by ISIS.

Provision of adequate police forces has been a long-standing challenge in Iraq. Development of police forces in Iraq, particularly those focused on community policing, had historically taken a backseat to development of military forces. Before the U.S. departure from Iraq in 2011, U.S. and Coalition training efforts focused overwhelmingly on army and special operations forces, including paramilitary police units, rather than on developing a sufficient number of competent federal police and local police forces.

The lack of police forces to secure the population effectively in major cities retaken from ISIS has been an acute issue. The Coalition had supported efforts to recall, recruit, and train security forces, including police. Non-U.S. coalition members, and particularly Italy's Carabinieri, had taken the lead in training police, due to U.S. restrictions on using its military to train police forces and legal requirements to vet trainees for any history of human rights abuses.

Canadian brigadier Dave Anderson, the top Coalition officer for the effort to train and equip Iraqi Security Forces and advise the security ministries, provided an overview of efforts to raise police forces as part of the $2.5 billion in military assistance

[35] Interview with National Security Service spokesman Saeed al-Jaishy, Baghdad, Iraq, February 2017.

provided since 2015.[36] His office developed and delivered a 2.5-year plan for restoring order in the five conflict-affected provinces to the Iraqi prime minister in February 2017. In that plan, the Coalition aimed to develop 25,000 police forces for Mosul, based on a ratio of 1 police officer for every 50 residents.

By April 2017, the Coalition had trained 13,000 police forces, including, by Anderson's count, 8,800 tribal forces and 2,600 new police. That meant at least 12,000 more police officers would need to be trained to provide adequate police capacity, as stipulated in the Coalition plan. To fulfill the goal of a locally recruited force, Anderson said 1,500 additional trainees were recruited from the IDP camps outside Mosul. The training program for police forces amounted to a total of six weeks: recruits received two weeks of training from the Ministry of Interior and four weeks of instruction from the Coalition. Tribal forces received even shorter training programs of one week to ten days, as they were designed to be temporary hold forces.

The Coalition recognized that the pace of police training was insufficient. To accelerate the output, it tripled the rate of training by increasing the number of Coalition trainers, which came from the Italian Carabinieri national police and the Canadian Royal Mounted Police. Spain's Garda Civil sent 25 trainers. This additional manpower would enable the Coalition to increase the output from 600 per month to 1,000 per month. However, even at that higher rate, producing the additional 16,700 police forces called for in the national plan would take almost a year and a half.

Policing infrastructure was also lacking in the cities that experienced the heaviest destruction. Canada supplied "police stations in a box," which consisted of trailers to serve as offices and two trucks. Canada also provided 100 "border posts in a box" as the borders with Syria and Jordan were secured.

Generating sufficient numbers was only part of the challenge; the quality and reputation of the forces were equally critical. Human rights groups have documented abuses by police forces, as well as heavily politicized control of the Ministry of Interior.[37] Anderson said that Interior Ministry officials acknowledged this problem. "They know they have it wrong. They know they lost the confidence of the people," he said. "They have embraced the idea of community-based policing," as well as the need to recruit locally. Nonetheless, the general noted problems with the hold force in Ramadi and Fallujah, including police officers shaking down residents and other corrupt acts. "I would give them a C–, not an F," he said. International NGOs such as IOM have small-scale programs aimed at developing community policing expertise among the newly trained police forces.

---

36 Interview with Canadian brigadier Dave Anderson, Baghdad, Iraq, February 2017.

37 Amnesty International, for example, has published numerous reports, most recently *Punished for Daesh's Crimes: Displaced Iraqis Abused by Militias and Government Forces*, New York, October 18, 2016.

Conclusion

This chapter surveys the security requirements for near-term stabilization of Mosul and the surrounding areas of Ninewa Province. The research conducted indicates that three issues are of particular importance. The first is the need to expand efforts to mitigate the extensive mine hazards that are impeding the return of civilians and stabilization activities that require a modicum of physical security. The second issue is the need to provide adequate hold forces to prevent ISIS from reinfiltrating cleared areas and waging attacks on returning civilians. The hold forces are likely to be drawn off to combat operations in Tal Afar, Hawija, and the Euphrates Valley following the Mosul offensive. This will open a dangerous gap in security for the cleared areas. The third issue is the need to increase the capacity of the police training program to produce more police more rapidly, with sufficient training to provide security. The Coalition has increased the number of international police trainers, largely supplied by Italy, Canada, and Spain, but additional trainers are needed to accelerate the throughput of the program. Additional training will be needed for those forces that have been lightly trained.

CHAPTER FOUR

Enabling Resumption of City Life

The resumption of city life in Mosul and the return of the displaced to their homes depends on a number of factors related to city public administration. These include public services, infrastructure, housing, and the economy. These factors are important for meeting the needs of civilians and also as tools for community trust, reconciliation, and reduction of tensions. One multilateral official observed, "People need to come back to their cities and find services so that they can stay. This is the best way to build trust in the government. There is a certain non-measureable factor, which is the trust and social contract which is being rebuilt."[1] This chapter describes considerations for improving these four factors related to resuming city life.

Public Services

Under ISIS, public services broke down as staff fled, policies and management changed, Baghdad cut off central government salaries to prevent ISIS from extorting them, and infrastructure was destroyed in the fighting.[2] These events particularly affected public utilities, health care, and education—all crucial for future city life and the return of the displaced.

Public Utilities (Water, Sanitation, and Electricity)

Under ISIS, Mosul experienced a significant decline in public utilities, including electricity, sanitation, and water.[3] The fighting to retake both East and West Mosul caused further utility infrastructure damage. Quickly rebuilding and restaffing utilities will be an important factor in enabling the resumption of city life and civilian returns. Utilities are also needed by firms, so the provision of them will be closely related to the economic revival of the city.

---

1 Telephone interview with multilateral official in Iraq, February 22, 2017.

2 UN-Habitat, 2016.

3 UN-Habitat, 2016.

City residents had access to electricity for only a few hours per day under ISIS. All electrical generating stations stopped functioning because of a lack of fuel; the electric grid was shut down for a period because of cracks in the Mosul dam; and ISIS controlled private generators. The city had lacked a wastewater system before ISIS, and parts of the city experienced floods of wastewater. Solid waste collection declined under ISIS, causing a buildup of street garbage. Water was not sterilized, and water treatment capacity was reduced by air raids, leaving water available only a few hours per day at arbitrary times. Residents purchased or filtered water for drinking, and water was often lacking for cleaning. In the fighting to take East Mosul, all five of Mosul's bridges were destroyed, which fractured the city's water system because the pipes ran under the bridges, according to UNICEF.[4]

To deal with the city water and electricity needs, UNICEF moved into East Mosul to develop water and sanitation service centers, and it engineered a pumping system with repairs to pipes. UNICEF trucked water into tanks and prepositioned centers with water, shower, latrines, and hygiene kits for 150,000 people. The UNDP prepositioned $11 million in supplies for rapid response in electricity, water, and municipal utilities.[5]

The need for investment in utilities will not be met by these stopgap emergency efforts to resume water and electricity. The World Bank has prioritized loans for rebuilding electricity, water, and transport quickly in other parts of Iraq. A senior World Bank official said that the bank was prepared to do the same in Mosul.[6] Indeed, across Iraq, 35 percent of Iraqi households believed that electricity should be the top priority for improvement, more than for any other sector.[7]

Health Care

Health services were severely degraded during ISIS's occupation.[8] Health care workers fled, for example, and 5,000 Mosul health care staff are now living in Erbil, according to the WHO.[9] Priority for medical care went to ISIS fighters instead of civilians. Gender segregation affected women's access to health care. Fees were imposed for previously free services. Medicines became less available. The WHO noted that 6 of Mosul's 12 hospitals were destroyed by January 2017; one hospital can cost $150 million. By April 2017, Mosul had only a quarter of its preconflict hospital capacity, with

---

4 Interview with UNICEF in Erbil, Iraq, January 2017.

5 UNDP in Iraq, 2016a, p. 3.

6 Telephone interview with multilateral official in Iraq, February 22, 2017.

7 UNDP in Iraq, "About Iraq," 2017. As of March 24, 2017: http://www.iq.undp.org/content/iraq/en/home/countryinfo.html.

8 UN-Habitat, 2016.

9 Interviews with WHO officials in Erbil, Iraq, January 2017.

800 out of its former 3,200 hospital beds operational. Basic services were neglected, as were routine immunization and care for chronic diseases.

This loss of health care infrastructure, health care institutional capacity, and facilities for ongoing and trauma needs in health care will be formidable challenges to address. The WHO and its partners started 59 mobile clinics in nearby communities, which cost $4.9 million, not including operations costs. The mobile clinics were necessary, as people were unable to go to regular clinics because of the risk of explosive hazards. UNICEF had teams ready to conduct a vaccination campaign against polio and measles.[10]

One UN official explained the importance of rapidly rebuilding hospitals: "Hospitals provide services, but they also represent peace and stability. They make people feel secure. Health care can be a means to bridge differences among sects."[11]

Education

When ISIS took Mosul in 2014, it closed all of the K–12 schools, changed the curriculum to represent its ideology, and then reopened the schools.[12] The quality of education declined, and ISIS charged fees for school attendance, which had previously been free. The combination of these factors led many parents to not send their children to school, causing a drop of school attendance. In Mosul and elsewhere occupied by ISIS, a million children either missed out on school or studied the ISIS curriculum.[13] Children were traumatized and indoctrinated; for example, Khazer I camp aid workers described children singing ISIS songs, relating atrocities that they had witnessed, and trying to enforce ISIS-directed social norms at the camp.[14]

ISIS shut down Mosul's universities, to reopen only departments related to medicine, engineering, and education later. ISIS executed many professors. Mosul University's administration opened up a temporary campus in Erbil. Located in East Mosul, much of the campus of Mosul University, once one of the most respected universities in Iraq, was destroyed in the fighting. Its buildings may have been used as chemical weapons production facilities and also barracks for ISIS fighters.[15]

---

[10] United Nations Iraq, "Unicef: Iraq Crisis Flash Update #1: Mosul Response 17–31 October 2016," November 2, 2016b. As of March 24, 2017: http://uniraq.org/index.php?option=com_k2&view=item&id=6278:unicef-iraq-crisis-flash-update-1-mosul-response-17-31-october-2016&Itemid=626&lang=en.

[11] Interviews with UN officials in Erbil, Iraq, January 2017.

[12] UN-Habitat, 2016.

[13] Lily Partland and Simon Edmunds, *Over a Million Children Living Under ISIS in Iraq Have Missed Out on Education: Save the Children*, Save the Children, November 6, 2016.

[14] Interviews with staff of Khazer I camp.

[15] "Mosul Battle: Iraq Forces 'Retake' University from IS," *BBC News*, January 14, 2017. As of March 24, 2017: http://www.bbc.com/news/world-middle-east-38623671.

Multiple interviewees noted that the lack of open K–12 schools and universities poses a barrier to IDPs returning home.[16] On the other hand, open schools and universities provide a powerful symbol of stability. For example, the reopening of Tikrit University was viewed as an important milestone and a signal that Tikrit was functioning and stable, and that civilians could return.[17]

Infrastructure

Closely intertwined with public service provision is infrastructure. A significant amount of infrastructure (both public and private) in Mosul was destroyed, both by ISIS during the occupation and by Coalition forces during the campaign to liberate Mosul. By August 2016, the United Nations estimated that 50 to 75 percent of Mosul's government infrastructure had been destroyed, and 60 to 75 percent of its manufacturing and industrial enterprises.[18] UN-Habitat found that a total of 877 sites were destroyed by January 2017: 419 housing sites, 228 roads, 106 commercial and industrial buildings, 37 public facilities in health and education, 55 public administration buildings, 21 military and security facilities, and 11 recreational facilities.[19] Electrical transformers and infrastructure were destroyed, as was the water network and Mosul's five bridges. All of the main sites of cultural heritage were destroyed, with some razed and turned into parking lots. As of January 2017, the majority of these destroyed sites were in East Mosul, with 157 of the sites in West Mosul. Within West Mosul, ISIS fighters built tunnels between houses and blocks and used churches, schools, and hospitals as storage areas for weapons caches. Given the narrow alleyways of West Mosul's older city sites, the fighting was expected to cause significant further damage.[20] Figure 4.1 illustrates infrastructure damage in Mosul as of January 2017. These estimates did not take into account additional damage inflicted during the latter phase of combat operations for West Mosul.

There were a number of efforts under way and opportunities for rebuilding destroyed or damaged infrastructure.

In one of the main efforts, the UNDP's FFIS and FFES funds have been used throughout Iraq in liberated areas. Prime Minister Haider al-Abadi tasked the governors of each of the five provinces impacted by ISIS, including Ninewa, with creat-

[16] Interview with Iraqi military official, UN official, and senior KRG official in Erbil, Iraq, January 2017.

[17] Judit Neurink, "Tikrit University Brings Life Back to Saddam's Hometown," *Rudaw*, June 6, 2016. As of May 1, 2017: http://www.rudaw.net/english/middleeast/iraq/060620161.

[18] UN-Habitat, 2016.

[19] UN-Habitat, *Mosul Data & Mapping Portal: Physical Damage Assessment*, January 31, 2017a.

[20] Ahmed Rasheed, "Islamic State Readies for Close Combat in Alleyways of West Mosul," Reuters, February 17, 2017. As of March 27, 2017: http://www.reuters.com/article/us-mideast-crisis-iraq-mosul-idUSKBN15W1GY.

Figure 4.1
Infrastructure Damage in Mosul

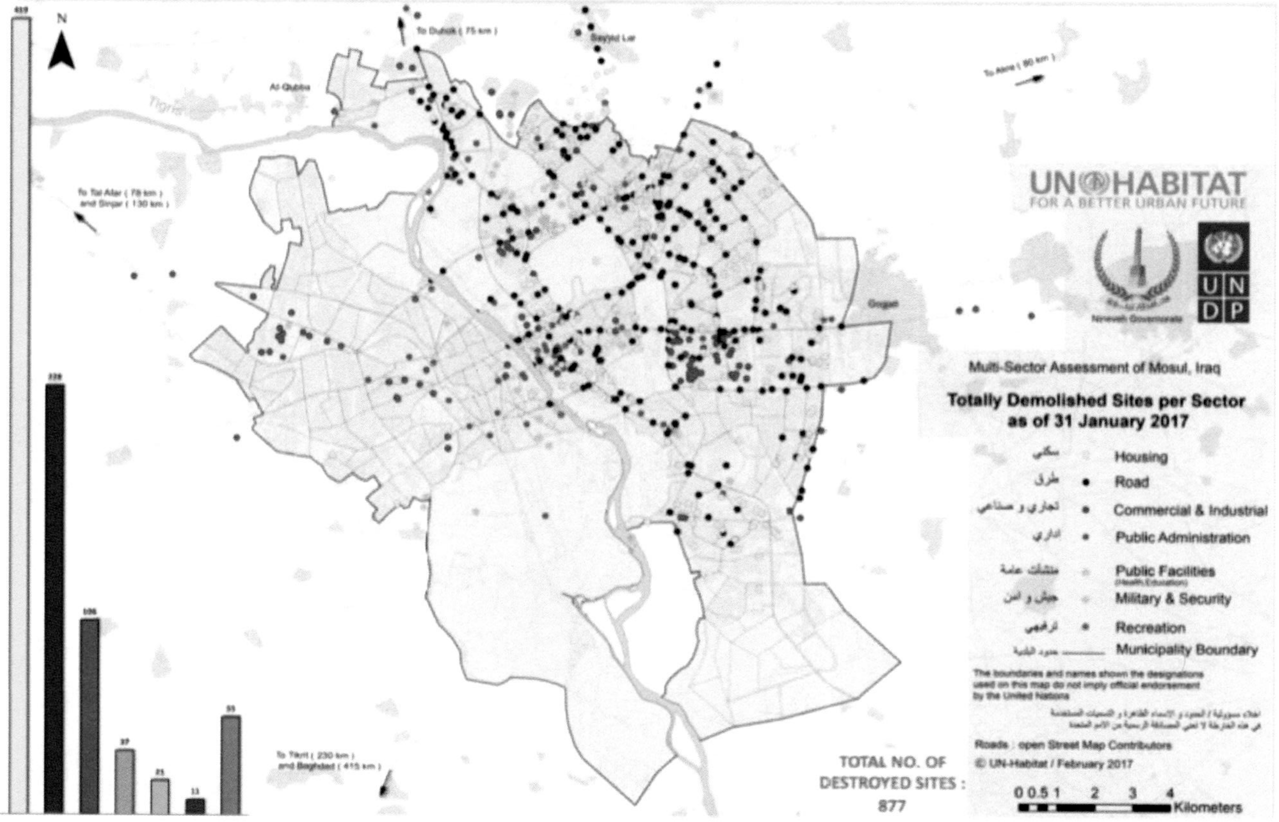

SOURCE: Graph provided for use by Un-Habitat in Erbil, Iraq.
RAND *RR2076-4.1*

ing a command cell of local notables. Command cells have temporary responsibilities in determining priorities for FFIS and FFES efforts in their province. Command cell members often included the military, police, regular and irregular security forces, imams, sheikhs, and wealthy community members. The command cells provided project proposals to the governor for UNDP funding and provided political buy-in; the cells co-opted "the people who could spoil stabilization," as described by one UN official. In Ninewa, the governor and command cell were slow in developing initial priorities due to political gridlock between the two entities.

With the assistance of USAID, Iraqi field technical teams surveyed liberated areas of Ninewa Province to determine the status of critical infrastructure and services and recommend early actions to the command cell.[21] As a result, power was restored to villages, and bridges in the Khazer, Qayarah, and Haji Ali villages were slated for early repair. Water infrastructure in villages was deemed relatively intact, but the box culverts on highways suffered extensive destruction.

The World Bank was also involved in reconstruction in Iraq. It budgeted $350 million in loans for the Iraqi government to rebuild after ISIS, with $200 million committed and $120 million contracted by February 2017. This funding was committed for Diyala, Salah al-Din, and Anbar provinces, and the World Bank would be available for loans to Ninewa Province when it became stable enough for assessments. World Bank loans supported water and sewage, municipal services and electricity, roads and bridges, and health services. Iraqi ministries identified the priorities and implemented the projects. The World Bank and UNDP coordinated on infrastructure building priorities in order to avoid duplication. Although the approach of implementing projects through Iraqi ministries built their capacity and addressed their priorities, it was often slowed down by decisionmaking processes in the ministries. Involvement in a conflict setting—taking risks to help a government in a fragile situation—was a new approach for the World Bank. Box 4.1 describes numerous lessons that were learned in the stabilization efforts that were mounted in Iraq's major cities after the military operations to dislodge ISIS.

Housing

Housing considerations will present a key problem for stabilization in Mosul for several reasons: the short supply of housing, the potential for improperly serviced neighborhoods to serve as incubators of radicalization, and the property ownership disputes that are likely to arise from ISIS's sale of property and destruction of ownership records.

Because of both the destroyed housing and preexisting housing shortages, Mosul will face the challenge of providing enough housing for its residents. ISIS destroyed

---

[21] USAID Iraq and Governance Strengthening Project—Taqadum, *Special Report on Ninewa: Post-Conflict Actions Taken in Liberated Areas*, September 2016.

many homes and left others heavily mined; those that survived ISIS have been damaged or destroyed by the battle to retake Mosul. Often, ISIS destroyed the housing of minorities and those who opposed it, leaving intact the homes of those who collaborated. This means that in some cases, it could be easier for ISIS sympathizers to return than for minorities or those who opposed ISIS. In other parts of Iraq, in Salah al-Din, Tikrit, and Anbar, 88 percent of IDPs displaced by ISIS were able to return to their original homes, while 12 percent could not because their homes were

Box 4.1 Lessons Learned in Resuming Services and Rebuilding from Tikrit, Ramadi, and Fallujah

In Salahhadin province, Tikrit was seen as a model for reconstruction and rebuilding efforts after liberation from ISIS. The Mayor of Tikrit and Prime Minister Abadi were credited with leading a well organized rebuilding effort, spearheading reopening of shops and food distribution centers.[22] The UNDP noted that the FFIS, under the leadership of the Tikriti Command Cell and the Governor, quickly developed a stabilization strategy and plan which resulted in the fast rehabilitation of the main water pumping station, the reopening of health centers, and reestablishment of the electricity network.[23] In Tikrit, the Iraqi government worked quickly to open bakeries and provided residents with rice and cooking oil.[24] The Mayor of Tikrit saw returning services and markets to civilians as critical to reassuring them that the area was safe for habitation, and therefore prioritized services and markets for emergency funding.

In contrast, rebuilding efforts in Ramadi were slower, due to the severe damage to the city during the drawn-out battle for control of the city. Nearly a year after Iraqi Security Forces retook the city, parts were still unlivable because of the large amounts of rubble still covering unexploded ordnance in critical areas like hospitals, schools, and houses.[25] Fallujah, unlike Ramadi, did not experience wide-scale devastation but still presented rebuilding challenges.[26] Ramadi and Fallujah both

---

[22] Tim Arango and Rick Gladstone, "Retaking Mosul from ISIS May Pale to What Comes Next," *New York Times*, October 18, 2016. As of March 16, 2017: https://www.nytimes.com/2016/10/19/world/middleeast/mosul-iraq-isis.html.

[23] UNDP in Iraq, "Tikrit: A Stabilization Success Following Liberation from ISIL," July 20, 2016b. As of March 27, 2017: http://www.iq.undp.org/content/iraq/en/home/ourwork/Stabilization/our-stories/stabilization-in-tikrit.html.

[24] Arango and Gladstone, 2016.

[25] Arango and Gladstone, 2016.

[26] Arango and Gladstone, 2016.

Box 4.1 Continued

fared worse than Tikrit when it came to providing emergency food supplies and access to markets. In Fallujah, road closures across Anbar province disrupted access to markets and created shortages of fresh produce, and exposed civilians to "extreme vulnerability" when they returned home.[27] A 2015 Shelter Cluster report estimated that "among displaced people, about 70 per cent report poor and borderline level food consumption scores in these areas [including Fallujah]."[28] The same report noted that markets were abandoned around Fallujah, which exacerbated food insecurity in the first months after liberation. In Ramadi, there were no functioning food markets for nearly eight months after the city was liberated from ISIS, requiring the Iraqi government to bring in food supplies during that period.[29] The slow return of markets to Ramadi, in particular, can be attributed to the generally high level of devastation of all major infrastructure in the city, requiring that the Iraqi government prioritize a general return of services and emergency food supplies over reopening markets.

In sum, the experiences of post-liberation stabilization in these three cities points to the importance of key steps: rubble clearing, investing in enabling markets and bakeries to function to provide access to food (including in ensuring available transportation to them), and prioritizing rebuilding of utilities and health clinics.

RAND *RR2076-box4.1*

destroyed or occupied by someone else, or conditions were too unsafe (e.g., the location was booby-trapped).[30]

Mosul had a housing shortage that predated ISIS: a deficit of 172,000 housing units in Ninewa overall, with a shortage of 53,000 units in Mosul. UN-Habitat attributes this to a failure to update Mosul's 1973 urban plan to allocate tracts of land for housing.[31] In addition, Mosul's population grew significantly after 2003; much of this expansion took place in illegal or informal settlements that had poor-quality housing and were insufficiently connected with city services.

---

27 UNOCHA, 2015.

28 UNOCHA, 2015.

29 REACH, *Assessment of Eight Hard-to-Reach Areas in Iraq, 2015–2016*, June 2016. As of March 27, 2017: https://www.sheltercluster.org/sites/default/files/docs/reach_irq_report_assessment_of_eight_hard-to-reach_areas_in_iraq_july_2016.pdf.

30 IOM: Iraq Mission, 2016b.

31 UN-Habitat, 2016.

Indeed, some of the insufficiently serviced informal settlements also became failed security zones. In Mosul, the leaders of Al-Qaeda in Iraq came primarily from three of these poorly serviced informal settlement neighborhoods: 17 Tamouz, Al-Eslah Al-Zerae, and Al-Nahrawan.[32] While there is an unsettled debate about the relationship between poverty and terrorism, a UN official pointed to an underappreciated correlation between these failed sections of the city and the incubation of radicalization: "Urban development and informal settlements are not taken seriously as a root cause of incubators, terrorism, and security challenges."[33] Analysis of causes of radicalization typically focuses on other factors; indeed, in this case, stabilization efforts should explicitly consider issues of equity in quality of life in order to create conditions for long-term stability.

Citywide property disputes related to housing are expected after combat operations. Such disputes have been a significant problem in other liberated parts of Iraq.[34] When Mosul residents fled in 2014, other IDPs and ISIS families moved into their houses. ISIS accessed property records in Mosul and used them to target minority-owned housing for confiscation, either giving them to ISIS fighters or selling them, as ISIS did in other parts of Iraq.[35] Property sales were a key way that ISIS raised revenue to support its operations.[36] ISIS also destroyed property records for home ownership in Mosul, although there may be remaining housing records in Baghdad.[37] House demolitions and property dispossession were barriers to returns home post-ISIS in other parts of Iraq.[38]

Economy

Mosul's economy significantly degraded under ISIS. Many businesses closed. Unemployment, inflation, and poverty rose. Many farmers stopped working because ISIS required them to sell at low, extortive prices. Two main areas of the Mosul city economy present challenges for stabilization: consumer goods markets (for goods required for daily needs, particularly food) and jobs.

Markets for consumer goods enable civilians to purchase food and essential items, they provide a space for public interaction, and they are a visible symbol of

---

32 UN-Habitat, 2016.

33 Telephone interview with UN official in Iraq, February 17, 2017.

34 IOM: Iraq Mission, 2016.

35 UN-Habitat, 2016; Internal Displacement Monitoring Centre, 2015.

36 UN-Habitat, 2016; Jane Arraf, "How Ramadi Was Won," *Newsweek*, February 22, 2016.

37 Internal Displacement Monitoring Centre, 2015.

38 Internal Displacement Monitoring Centre, 2015.

the resumption of normalcy. Markets in East Mosul emerged after military operations ended, with shops for food, clothing, cell phones, and more opening quickly.[39] A common theme among interviewees was that the resumption of city life in East Mosul was "better than anyone expected," in particular in comparison with the experiences of other liberated cities. Ramadi, for example, required government intervention in food supplies because markets did not reopen for eight months after liberation (see Box 4.1). Because of this experience, the FFIS prioritized assistance to markets reopening in other liberated cities, with particular success in Tikrit, where more than a hundred small businesses, including bakeries, grocers, and repair shops, received cash grants to start operating.[40]

An IOM survey found that after safety and the condition of their home, IDPs said that the most important factor enabling them to return home was the availability of their livelihood.[41] Availability of jobs or self-employment to make a living will be key to enabling civilians to stay. Job creation will need to be focused on both the short term and longer term.

In terms of short-term opportunities, public-sector workers have the ability to resume their jobs, with salaries through Baghdad. Employing youth to remove rubble has been one FFIS approach in other cities that created jobs and the conditions needed for others to return.[42] Reconstruction could also provide job opportunities; experiences from other liberated cities found that access to rebuilt roads and bridges was also key for the resumption of trade.

In terms of longer-term jobs, the current heavy reliance on the Iraqi government to provide jobs may not be sustainable. The government provides 40 percent of jobs in Iraq.[43] With the low price of oil and Iraq's financial crisis, the government cannot continue to be the primary employer, as a multilateral agency official noted.[44] Jobs would depend on the private sector. However, encouraging the private sector depends first on security, said the multilateral official, and next on other measures to build the confidence of investors in agriculture, trade, manufacturing, hotels and tourism, and the oil

---

[39] Rupert Jones, "News Transcript: Department of Defense Press Briefing by Maj. Gen. Jones via Teleconference from Baghdad, Iraq," U.S. Department of Defense, February 15, 2017. As of March 27, 2017: https://www.defense.gov/News/Transcripts/Transcript-View/Article/1084947/department-of-defense-press-briefing-by-maj-gen-jones-via-teleconference-from-b?source=GovDelivery; Reuters, "Mosul's East Begins to Bustle but Healing a Long Way Off," *New York Times*, March 24, 2017. As of March 28, 2017: https://www.nytimes.com/reuters/2017/03/24/world/middleeast/24reuters-mideast-crisis-iraq-mosul-residents.html?_r=0.

[40] UNDP in Iraq, 2016b.

[41] IOM: Iraq Mission, 2016a.

[42] UNDP in Iraq, 2016a.

[43] UNDP in Iraq, 2017.

[44] Telephone interview with multilateral official in Iraq, February 22, 2017; telephone interview with UN official in Iraq, February 13, 2017.

industry. This will be a particular challenge in Mosul, where most of the factories that provided jobs have been destroyed. Iraq needs to reform its state-centric and antiquated legal and regulatory environment to spur its business environment, rather than continuing on a path of state-directed economy.

Conclusion

Resuming city life in Mosul will depend on a set of immediate steps that involve restarting public services, repairing or rebuilding key public infrastructure, developing a process to deal with property disputes so that people whose homes were given away or sold by ISIS can return, and jump-starting Mosul's economy with consumer goods markets and jobs. The goal of stabilization is not to create long-term plans in these domains. Rather, it is to implement a set of immediate steps that enable Moslawis to live with a minimum basic standard of living, that remove additional reasons for conflict arising from scarcity, and that provide conditions for IDPs to return to their homes, communities, and jobs.

CHAPTER FIVE

Governance and Political Reconciliation

This chapter examines the governance considerations and political conflicts that need to be addressed to achieve long-term stability in Mosul and, by extension, all of Iraq.[1] The chapter focuses on two issues related to the post-ISIS stabilization effort at both the local and national levels: first, building effective governing capacity, and second, achieving reconciliation in order to resolve the political conflicts that threaten to make Iraq a permanently failed state.

Governance issues involve reconstituting governing capacity in Mosul and Ninewa, as well as improving the national government's overall ability to deliver services to provinces. A major initiative that spans both levels is decentralization. Iraq's constitution allows for a process of decentralization, and Iraq's parliament passed a provincial powers law in 2008 and revised it in 2013 to devolve the functions of eight ministries to the provinces. Decentralization is intended to improve service delivery and address political desires for greater local control.

Reconciliation is another requirement for successful stabilization, and progress is needed at both the local and national levels. Conflict resolution and similar measures are needed at the local level to stitch communities back together, and deliberate efforts are needed at the national level to resolve core political disputes. As Iraq's largest Sunni-majority city, Mosul's political leaders are participants at both the local and national levels. For example, Osama Nujaifi, brother of the former governor of Ninewa, is one of Iraq's vice presidents and leader of a political party. Top-down and bottom-up reconciliation efforts are mutually reinforcing, though pursued through different types of programs and initiatives. Conversely, in the absence of a national impetus for reconciliation, local leaders may be reluctant to take the risks entailed in knitting their communities back together.

The chapter starts by describing the backdrop of the Sunni-Shia political conflict in Iraq, then discusses the post-ISIS challenges for governing Ninewa and how

---

[1] *Governance* is defined in U.S. military doctrine as "the state's ability to serve the citizens through the rules, processes, and behavior by which interests are articulated, resources are managed, and power is exercised in a society, including the representative participatory decision-making processes typically guaranteed under inclusive, constitutional authority." Joint Publication 1-02.

they relate to the overall architecture for governing Iraq. Energizing the slow efforts to implement Iraq's decentralization law holds promise for improving the quality of government at the local level and thus easing the overall tension between Sunni and Shia political blocs. Reconciliation efforts have been similarly moribund, despite small-scale programming at the local level and United Nations efforts at the national level. Without greater progress and a clear road map for post-ISIS governance and reconciliation in Ninewa, and more broadly at the national level, the success of efforts to stabilize Iraq may be in jeopardy. Conversely, progress in Mosul and among the national political parties—which include significant Mosul figures—will spur confidence in the country's ability to forge a gradual path to peace.

Overcoming a Bitter Legacy

The ISIS threat is rooted in the larger Iraqi political conflict that bedeviled the country since Saddam Hussein was overthrown by the U.S. intervention in 2003. The majority of ISIS fighters in Iraq were drawn from Iraq's Sunni population, which has lost much of its status under Shia-majority rule since Saddam Hussein's dictatorship was overthrown. The Shia-led government of Nuri al-Maliki pursued a sectarian agenda, and incidents such as a violent response to Sunni protests in Hawija in 2013 fueled the Sunni drift into ISIS arms. Thousands of Sunnis languished in jail, and many were branded by a de-Baathification law that denied them job opportunities.

The violence perpetrated by ISIS greatly exacerbated these divisions, as the latest and most viral form of the insurgent jihadist movement representing the most extreme manifestation of Sunni discontent. Sunnis have suffered greatly at ISIS hands as well. According to UN and U.S. officials, the majority of the 3 million displaced were Sunnis, and many of the estimated 10 million affected by the violence are also Sunni.[2] The Shia majority, also victimized by ISIS attacks, was loath to fund reconstruction of Sunni areas without assurances that attacks emanating from those areas would permanently cease.

These severe internal rifts were further exacerbated by the interests and activities of regional neighbors. The degree of Iranian influence and involvement in Iraqi internal affairs greatly concerned the surrounding Arab states, most of all Saudi Arabia, which is locked in a pitched contest with Iran over Yemen. The Arab states view Iranian influence in Iraq as part of Iran's bid to extend its sway through Iraq, Syria, and Lebanon. Iran's Revolutionary Guard Corps provides aid, arms, and senior-level advis-

---

2 Interviews with UN and U.S. officials in Erbil, Iraq, January 2017, and Baghdad, February 2017.

ers to the Iraqi government and powerful Iraqi militias, and it had persuaded Iraqi militias to fight on behalf of the Syrian regime in that country.[3]

As a result of Iran's heavy role in Iraq, the Gulf States had been halting in their assistance to the government, even though such assistance would benefit the Iraqi Sunni population. UN and U.S. officials we interviewed noted that difficulties in obtaining funding from the Gulf States for stabilization arose because of the countries' concerns about indirectly supporting Iran.[4] Turkey had also supported various Sunni factions in Iraq, including training Sunni militias (such as the militia affiliated with former Ninewa governor Atheel Nujaifi), and supporting the KRG.

Although ISIS appeared on its way to suffering a decisive military defeat as of mid-2017, the danger existed that ISIS or its successor would continue to gain traction in Sunni areas if the long-standing grievances, core issues surrounding the division of power and the architecture of the state in Iraq, and local desires for self-governance and quality of life were not resolved. The KRG was a significant additional factor in this power struggle, as many Kurds shared the anti-Sunni Arab sentiments of the Shia Arab Iraqi majority due to the atrocities and repression they suffered under Saddam Hussein.

Stabilizing Mosul was thus part of a much broader issue, namely, determining the place of Sunni Arabs in the new Iraq. The 2005 constitution and provincial powers legislation contained the basic elements to resolve it: the creation of a more federal union that gave provinces and regions the power to oversee their own affairs. Implementation of Iraq's decentralization 2013 law was halting, but it held the prospect for an eventual reordering of the state. Kurds aspired to create their own state, which created another source of uncertainty, but they had achieved a measure of autonomy under their regional government status. This arrangement was underwritten by an agreement with the central government, enshrined in the annual budget law since 2008, to share 17 percent of federal revenues with the KRG. The inability of the Shia majority to reach an accommodation with the Sunni population stems in part from the repression suffered under Saddam Hussein, but also from infighting and power struggles among the four main Shia political parties. These national-level dynamics will determine the policies adopted toward Ninewa and other liberated areas.

---

[3] Iran's activities are detailed in the forthcoming study: Linda Robinson, Todd Helmus, Raphael Cohen, Ali Nader, Andrew Radin, Madeline Magnuson, and Katya Migacheva, *Modern Political Warfare: Current Practices and Possible Responses*, Santa Monica, Calif.: RAND Corporation, forthcoming.

[4] Interviews with U.S. officials, Washington, D.C., December 2016, and UN officials in Iraq via telephone, March 2017.

Governing Ninewa After ISIS

Successful stabilization of Mosul, to include the resumption of public services, the further development of local governance, and the reparation of the torn social fabric, will require competent government supported by the population. The most urgent governance issues to be addressed are the following: who will govern Ninewa, the structure of Ninewa Province's government, and ensuring adequate administrative capacity. Western diplomats, the KRG, and others had urged Baghdad to reach early decisions on at least the mechanism for determining Ninewa's political governance. However, the central government decided to postpone this until the military operations to retake Ninewa had concluded.

The current Ninewa governor, Nawful Hamadi Sultan, hailed from Ninewa Province rather than Mosul. His selection by the Provincial Council was an interim move to sidestep competition among Moslawi factions after governor Atheel Nujaifi was forced out on corruption charges. Nujaifi is the brother of Osama Nujaifi, one of Iraq's vice presidents.[5] Several diplomats and international officials who have dealt with Ninewa's governor criticized his slowness in taking charge of the urgent stabilization tasks.[6] He failed to approve projects as required under the UNDP's FFIS program, so the senior Baghdad official overseeing the process, Mahdi al-Alaq, the acting secretary general of the Council of Ministers, assumed authority for approval of projects in Ninewa. Frustrated with the governor's inaction, international officials and diplomats began working directly with the directors general of the national line ministries in Ninewa and with the local district officials in order to approve an additional 200 critical humanitarian and stabilization projects for Ninewa. On the other hand, one Western official noted strengths of the governor, including generally behaving with decency, valuing Western advising, and developing a growing track record of accomplishments, such as playing an important role in enabling the resumption of work and life in Qayarah by helping to rehabilitate the water lines and restart operations at the oil refinery.[7]

Although Iraqi provincial elections for governors had been slated for April 2017, the Iraqi government postponed these until April 2018. Among the options noted by our interviewees as possible contenders for the role of Ninewa governor were the current governor, a notable Moslawi such as Osama Nujaifi, or former defense minister Khalid Obaidi, who hailed from Mosul.[8] Options such as a military governor appeared

---

[5] Dan DeLuce and Henry Johnson, "Who Will Rule Mosul?," *Foreign Policy*, April 29, 2016. As of March 27, 2017: http://foreignpolicy.com/2016/04/29/iraq-isis-sunni-shiite-kurds-fight-mosul/.

[6] Telephone interview with UN official in Iraq, February 13, 2017; interview with U.S. officials in Washington, D.C., December 13, 2016.

[7] Interviews with UN and U.S. officials in Erbil, Iraq, January 2017, and in Baghdad, February 22, 2017.

[8] Interview with Western official in Erbil, Iraq, January 2017.

less likely, though an interim consortium representing tribes and key figures from Mosul and the Ninewa plains was possible.

Equally important will be ensuring a fully representative governing structure for Ninewa Province. Some suggested dividing the province into three areas: western Ninewa, where Turkmen and other minorities are prevalent, although the devastated Yazidi population would face a struggle to return and rebuild; Mosul and the largely Sunni southern districts; and the Ninewa plains areas, where Christians and other minorities had settled. Others suggested moving toward the formation of a semiautonomous region similar to the Kurdistan Region, as permitted by the constitution.[9] The former scheme would not likely be acceptable to Sunnis, as it would greatly reduce their sway over a large province they have historically dominated. The latter scheme would face resistance from the aforementioned minorities, whose experiences of atrocities under Sunni ISIS fighters have made them fear continued rule by their Sunni neighbors.

KRG influence was likely to remain strong in eastern Ninewa Province, as the peshmerga and police exerted de facto control, but both Baghdad and the Sunnis of Ninewa could be reluctant to formalize this arrangement. The KRG could continue to provide security through its peshmerga in the short term, while formal governance remained Sunni dominated.

Finally, the physical infrastructure and governing capacity had been badly degraded by ISIS, war, and the fleeing of key staff. According to a UN-Habitat report, between one-half and three-quarters of Mosul's governmental buildings were destroyed as of 2016.[10] Additional damage occurred during the 2017 offensive to retake the city.

Municipal staffing of public-sector institutions will be an acute challenge in resuming public administration. Many employees fled, and those who remained are likely to be treated with suspicion due to their continued work under ISIS's rule. ISIS brought in foreigners to lead some administrative functions but kept locals as staff. At the same time, UN officials noted that these government employees did not necessarily support ISIS, even if they and many Mosul residents had low levels of support for Iraq's national government or Ninewa's provincial government. Excluding current employees on the assumption that they were allies of ISIS would be "extremely dangerous," noted one UN official; it could lead to the same mistakes (such as de-Baathification) that previously fueled discontent. "This is the most complicated thing to start stabilization of the city," said one UN official.[11] The governor of Ninewa believed that a fair process could

---

9 Former governor Atheel Nujaifi made these statements, as reported by Turkish and Kurdish media. See Mewan Dolmari, "Nineveh to Be Divided into Eight Provinces: Former Governor," *Kurdistan24*, September 8, 2016. As of March 19, 2017: http://www.kurdistan24.net/en/news/2e0926ae-87ad-4a8b-a39e-60b9bcc6baec/Nineveh-to-be-divided-into-eight-provinces—Former-Governor.

10 UN-Habitat, 2017b.

11 Telephone interview with UN official in Iraq, February 17, 2017.

be developed to vet government employees from Mosul via security databases by checking whether employees were members of ISIS and, if so, investigating them for possible crimes.

Decentralization: Challenges and Promise

A functional government in Ninewa Province will not be sufficient to provide for residents' needs. Iraq's highly centralized government means that plans, decisions, and services supplied by Baghdad will critically affect the prospects for stability in the provinces. Allegations of corruption, a lack of accountability, and perceived neglect of Sunni areas are all governance issues that involve the national government and require its action. Corruption has become a major rallying point in recent years, spurring protests across Iraqi society. Nationwide protests erupted in 2015, and Shia politician Muqtada al-Sadr instigated a mass incursion in the government Green Zone district of Baghdad. Prime Minister Haider al-Abadi responded to the mass protests by reducing the size of government and proposing a laundry list of reforms, but he lacked the support in parliament to implement changes. Corruption charges were leveled against numerous senior officials, and the parliament removed a number of ministers. The World Bank has initiated programs to improve public management, and it has tied its funding to performance standards. Under Dr. Naufel al-Hassan, the central government is attempting to improve the transparency and accountability of public finances.

Another avenue through which governance might be improved is decentralization. Iraq's Article 45, Law 21, the Provincial Power Act of 2013, devolved the functions of eight ministries to provinces.[12] Officials working in the effort view this initiative as a means to improve service delivery and garner greater citizen support for a government that performs better. The theory was that local government could be more responsive to citizens' needs, and the closer the government was to the people, the more they would support it. "If you make traction in these areas, that is the beginning of nonsectarian politics," a UN official said. "This is now breaking the cycle of grievances, allowing people to develop the compact with their societies."[13]

However, implementation of this law has been slow because government ministries are a major source of patronage, the central government oversight commission meets only six times a year to make decisions, war with ISIS distracted management attention, and Iraq had a long-standing tradition of centralized government. The Finance Ministry balked at devolution of its functions, and the progress to date con-

[12] The ministries are municipalities and public works; construction and housing; labor and social affairs; education; health; agriculture; finance; and sports and youth. The Iraqi government decided against decentralization of finance ministry functions, at least for the time being.

[13] Telephone interview with UN official in Iraq, February 13, 2017.

sisted largely of opening bank accounts to permit three ministries (education, health, and agriculture) to begin functioning as provincial entities. The World Bank was also working with the Iraqi government on fiscal decentralization.[14] The process of analyzing ministerial functions, mapping the devolution process, and making decisions about the functions to be devolved involved hundreds of officials in training and consultative sessions, supported by a USAID program called the Governance Strengthening Project—Taqadum. The two-year project, slated to conclude in September 2017, produced detailed plans and a modicum of capacity for financial processes, legal regulations, organizational development, and service delivery. A pilot implementation of a new trash-collection method doubled the service efficiency and increased citizen satisfaction by 80 percent.[15]

Fully implementing decentralization will take a decade, according to an implementer in the Taqadum program.[16] Progress toward decentralization in Ninewa would require settling the issue of who is to govern the province, as well as decisions about staffing. The USAID implementer believed that the decentralization program could be successful if the discontented and the youth of Iraq came to embrace it as part of their protest objectives. The implementer noted, "Decentralization is the solution for a lot of problems."

Reconciliation at the Local Level

The liberation of Mosul represents an important opportunity to foster local reconciliation, as residents have emerged from two and half years of brutal repression under ISIS. The military successes, unprecedented collaboration between the Iraqi Security Forces and the KRG peshmerga in fighting ISIS, and relatively professional behavior of the security forces (including the Shia PMF) represented an important opportunity to build on. A Baghdad official noted that government tip lines were jammed with calls from citizens seeking to report on ISIS movements as the offensive gained traction. A Western diplomat convened a civil society discussion for Mosul residents, and the participants expressed gratitude for the Iraqi military. A large billboard in East Mosul publicly thanked the Counter-Terrorism Service for its role in liberating the city. Iraqi aid groups supplied humanitarian assistance.

Nonetheless, many aid workers and diplomats noted that the level of violence, displacement, and trauma, and the ongoing deep grievances on all sides, tempered the

---

14 World Bank, *Republic of Iraq: Decentralization and Subnational Service Delivery in Iraq: Status and Way Forward*, March 2016. As of March 27, 2017: http://documents.worldbank.org/curated/en/583111468043159983/pdf/Iraq-Decentralization-JIT-Assessment-Report-March-2016-FINAL.pdf.

15 USAID Iraq and Governance Strengthening Project—Taqadum, 2016.

16 Interview with U.S. contractor and implementer in Erbil, Iraq, January 16, 2017.

prospects for rapid progress in this realm. Representatives of the Yazidi and Christian minorities told us that they feared returning to their home communities and preferred to seek asylum abroad or emigrate.[17] Some Iraqis feared they would be targeted as collaborators by Iraqi or KRG security forces or militias; minority communities also feared their Sunni Arab neighbors, whom they viewed as complicit in the atrocities of ISIS.[18] Although the degree of support for ISIS within Mosul was unknown, delayed services and remediation of the many problems could lead to rising discontent among the fearful Sunnis. After two years under ISIS rule, many children and youth were indoctrinated with extremist ideas and trained as militants.

A variety of small-scale efforts at local reconciliation have begun, though they are not widely coordinated or centrally planned. In Ninewa Province, a council of about 80 community leaders was created to address three issues regarding future reconciliation in Ninewa: the future of the Yazidis, tribal divisions among the Sunni and Shia Turkmen tribes, and tribal differences among the Arab tribes. The governor of Ninewa noted that he had met repeatedly with Yazidi leaders to discuss a plan for reconciliation; he planned to create a publicity campaign in Ninewa to communicate that Sunni Arabs there did not agree with ISIS's treatment of Yazidi women, as he believed it was not permitted by Islam or by Arab culture.[19]

The United States has also backed a number of reconciliation efforts. A widely noted success was the work of the U.S. Institute of Peace (USIP) and local NGO Sana, which brokered reconciliation among Shia and Sunni residents in Tikrit in Salah al-Din Province, where up to 1,700 Shia air force cadets were massacred by ISIS fighters. USIP had teams of local Iraqi facilitators who were experienced in conflict resolution and had conducted work in hot spots other than Tikrit in five provinces, in Kirkuk, Anbar, Diyala, and Ninewa Province. Their work was coordinated with the United Nations as well as the Iraqi government. The U.S. embassy was also considering new programs to address the trauma suffered by Iraqis on an individual level; the extreme brutality they suffered was considered a major impediment to security and stability at the community level.

The UNDP stabilization facilities FFIS and FFES included small social cohesion programs, but U.S. officials acknowledged that much more needed to be done on this front. One of four categories or "windows" of the UN-administered FFIS is for such projects. The U.S. embassy official in charge of future programming stated that these efforts should be emphasized more in the FFIS, the FFES, and other program vehicles.

---

[17] Interview with NGO and settlement officials, Erbil, Iraq, January 18, 2017.

[18] In earlier clearance operations in eastern Ninewa Province and Kirkuk, the Human Rights Watch reported that peshmerga burned the homes of Sunnis to prevent them from returning. The majority of allegations have been lodged against the Shia militias and, to a lesser extent, the Iraqi Security Forces. Intertribal violence has also been reported between those Sunni communities that supported and opposed ISIS.

[19] Telephone interview with Governor Nawful Hamadi Sultan in Erbil, Iraq, March 17, 2017.

In 2017, the UNDP initiated a three-part nationwide program to facilitate reconciliation and social cohesion: a national mass media campaign to educate the public on the benefits and urgency of reconciliation; the provision of funding to civil society groups to organize local community gatherings to discuss local divisions and how to overcome them; and a national memory project designed to collect accounts of atrocities and abuses. Such accounts could also serve a future transitional justice effort that might be part of a national reconciliation agreement. These efforts were instrumental in aiding South Africa in its passage from the apartheid era to full democracy. IOM also ran programs aimed at fostering community policing concepts in Ninewa, where citizens and police worked together to address neighborhood problems.

National Reconciliation

The divisions that have torn apart Ninewa Province are the same issues that divide the country at large. Given Mosul's prominence as Iraq's largest Sunni city, it is unlikely that it will be stabilized by actions taken only at the local level. Numerous international diplomats also noted that efforts to prioritize stabilization in one area over others would likely sow conflict. Given the bitter divisions among Iraq's constituent groups, some observers have grown skeptical that any effort to reach a national agreement among the Shia, Sunni, and Kurdish leaders of political parties might bear fruit. Others believe that the costs of continued conflict and the prospect of renewed war merit continued effort.

A major element of the United Nations Assistance Mission for Iraq is to support inclusive political development and national reconciliation, and to that end it has sought to foster talks among the major political groups. A breakthrough appeared possible in the fall of 2016, when Shia parties reached agreement on a document calling for reconciliation in the wake of ISIS's defeat. According to a diplomat involved in the talks, the document was to be presented to Sunni leaders in order to initiate cross-party talks.[20] The document was not to be publicized, but the leader of the Shia bloc, the Iraqi National Alliance, leaked the document to the press. Other Shia parties and political leaders backed away from it.[21] Furthermore, the Iraqi parliament passed the law making the PMF a formal legal entity. Sunni groups had hoped that this largely Shia armed entity (only 9,000 of 110,000 forces are Sunni) would be disbanded or individual troops migrated into the army and police forces if they passed a professional vetting process and were severed from their political (and in many cases Iranian-backed) leadership. The formalization of the PMF torpedoed the national reconciliation (alternatively

[20] Telephone interview with UN official in Baghdad, March 15, 2017.

[21] Ali Mamouri, "Is It Time for a National Settlement in Iraq?," *Al-Monitor*, November 9, 2016. As of March 27, 2017: http://www.al-monitor.com/pulse/en/originals/2016/11/national-reconciliation-iraq-shiite-kurd-sunni.html.

called the national settlement) talks: The Sunni leaders said that they would not consider the document unless changes were made in the PMF law.[22]

An international diplomat lamented that since this meeting in December 2016, the initiative has passed to Sunni expatriate groups outside Iraq and regional backers such as Saudi Arabia, Qatar, and Turkey, depriving those inside Iraq with the leadership role he believed they should have.[23] A meeting held in Turkey in March 2017 also resulted in a repudiation of a draft Sunni document, signaling the ongoing rejectionist stance by Iraq's highly divided Sunni community. Sunnis long espoused a set of similar demands, but they were unwilling to unite around a written proposal and a clear leader, as they jockeyed among themselves for position and to avoid being tainted by charges of selling out. This dissension was matched on the Shia side by posturing for the upcoming elections in 2018. Several diplomats engaged in the reconciliation discussions stated that an essential prerequisite is for Sunni leaders to articulate a common set of objectives, so that the UN can provide technical assistance to shape an approach to dialogue. One frustrated diplomat said, "The Sunnis cannot see the larger picture and take a long-term perspective. It is always the micro-issues that keep them from coming together."[24] Fearing that they would suffer the same fate as the marginalized Christian community, this official said he warned Sunni political leaders that they were squandering what could be their last opportunity.

Multiple officials believed that it is essential to establish a sustained process of ongoing national-level talks and confidence-building measures. A UN official said, "Here in Iraq the sides only talk when they are forming a government. Nothing is discussed after they pick and confirm the ministers."[25] This process is also essential to give impetus to the local leaders and citizens to come together, he argued. Without a process under way, citizens or local leaders will not take risks or act as though they have a stake in the state. The initiation of a process will require leadership from both the Shia and Sunni communities. A Sunni adviser to the Speaker of parliament, Salim al-Jabouri, said the Speaker represented a new generation of leadership, but he acknowledged that his party, the Iraqi Islamic Party, was one of the least popular Sunni factions.[26]

The danger of entropy in the wake of the military operations to clear Mosul could motivate parties inside and outside Iraq to push for a road map document that could at least form the basis for convening talks. Without forward movement before elections, past precedent suggests that talks to form a new government, name a prime minister,

---

[22] Omar Sattar, "How Iraq's PMU Law Is Disrupting National Unity Efforts," *Al Monitor*, December 14, 2016. As of March 27, 2017: http://www.al-monitor.com/pulse/originals/2016/12/national-settlement-pmu-law-iraq.html#.

[23] Telephone interview with UN official in Baghdad, March 15, 2017.

[24] Telephone interview with UN official in Baghdad, March 15, 2017.

[25] Telephone interview with UN official in Baghdad, March 15, 2017.

[26] Telephone interview with UN official in Iraq, February 13, 2017.

and divide up the cabinet positions could take many months if not a year. The valuable momentum provided by military progress could be squandered, and Sunni discontent could emerge shortly after.

A number of international, U.S., and Iraqi officials stated that the United States possesses significant leverage by virtue of the extensive military and nonmilitary aid it has provided. The previous U.S. administration chose to focus on day-to-day management of the relationship and the counter-ISIS campaign. However, the majority of interlocutors interviewed believe that Iraqis will not be able to chart a forward path on reconciliation without significant impetus from key international backers. A senior KRG official urged the U.S. government to become more active in pushing for a national settlement and wielding carrots and sticks to encourage progress. "I think the Americans should do more than they are. Iraqis need them," the minister said. "[The Americans] should use their influence more. Japan is giving loans to Iraq, on the condition that 17 percent of those loans must go to the KRI [Kurdistan Region of Iraq]." He noted that Baghdad complied with this condition.[27]

A diplomat in Baghdad noted that some Sunni leaders hoped that the United States would champion their cause out of a dislike for Iranian-backed Iraqi politicians. While Iran's influence is certainly strong, the path to a much-needed political accommodation may not be through the adoption of an advocacy role but rather through the support of a process that will recognize and remedy the need for due process, accountability, and good-faith compromises. At the end of the day, any national settlement would have to be agreed on by a majority of the Shia political actors, and U.S. leverage could best be applied to narrow the gaps between the two sides.

Conclusion

Success in Mosul cannot occur without progress at both the national and local levels on governance and reconciliation. Decentralization is a key demand of Moslawis and Sunnis, and it is the only part of their wish list that has actually made it into law. Thus, it is one key part of the political steps needed to stabilize Mosul and the wider Sunni belt. Reconciliation is very much part of the conversation as well, as the decisions about post-ISIS political representation in Ninewa will begin the process of sorting out Sunni national-level leadership in advance of elections. The post-Mosul period is a critical time for making some progress in at least defining the road map of issues for what will likely be an extended dialogue that might not formally start until after the 2018 elections. More ominously, senior UN officials are worried that stasis will lead to a slide back into full insurgency (as opposed to a less potent phase of ISIS dead-enders).

---

[27] Interview with senior KRG official, January 2017.

CHAPTER SIX

Conclusion and Recommendations

In surveying the humanitarian and stabilization effort in Iraq, we discovered many positive results and promising initiatives. Iraq and the Coalition actively sought to minimize civilian casualties. Iraq, with UN support and Coalition funding, carried out humanitarian and stabilization programs. Aid was delivered in conflict zones and in IDP camps. Major conflict was avoided among host communities and IDPs. Substantial Baghdad–Kurdistan Region military and humanitarian cooperation was achieved. And lessons learned (such as the need for professional checkpoints and donor investment in restarting bakeries) were applied from earlier phases of the response.

However, given the staggering costs and suffering imposed by the war, recovery and stability in Mosul will only be possible with redoubled efforts by Iraqis, as well as the international community. The following list of recommendations (summarized in Figure 6.1) was developed to identify priority areas for improved responses over the next twelve months regarding (1) urgent humanitarian actions; (2) expanded stabilization; (3) governance and reconciliation, including addressing the highly complex and intractable political divisions that remain a root cause of Iraq's conflict; and (4) cross-cutting issues.

Full recovery in Mosul, as in Iraq's other conflict-affected areas, will likely take a decade or more, given the levels of physical destruction and wounds to the social fabric in communities. But in the coming months the Iraqi government, with international support, must provide for Iraqis' basic needs, fulfill the requirement for safety and security, and lay the groundwork for resolving the political drivers of conflict in a sustainable manner. Without a practicable scheme for progressively addressing these fundamental issues, along with increased efforts by the Iraqi government, the Coalition, and humanitarian actors, there is good reason to expect that another wave of violence could ensue in Mosul and elsewhere in Iraq in a matter of months. The timeframes specified are the recommended windows for making substantial progress to build on the momentum gained through the military successes and to forestall major suffering, popular discontent, and the reinfiltration of ISIS into cleared areas. Completion of these recommended actions will in many cases require continued attention.

These recommendations are intended to be implemented not by a single actor but rather as a collective endeavor by the primary stakeholders: the government of Iraq, the

Figure 6.1
Recommendations

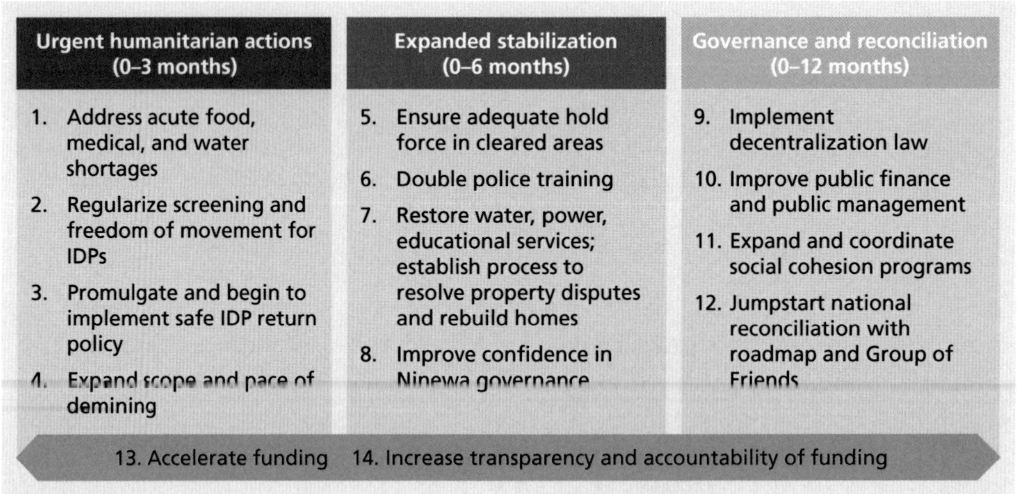

RAND *RR2076-6.1*

United States and other members of the Coalition, and the United Nations, with other international and nongovernmental organizations. Possible burden-sharing schemes are suggested for specific recommendations. While additional funding will be required, the most urgent needs can be met by accelerating the delivery of funds already promised and through active leadership, diplomacy, and coordination. The additional financial burden can and should be shared among those with direct interests in a stable Iraq. As oil prices recover, the government of Iraq can shoulder an increasing burden, and improved financial management will produce increasingly cost-effective returns. The primary requirement for the United States is to embrace a long-term approach, endorse the needed measures, supply expertise, and exercise leadership in this critical phase of winning the peace.

Urgent Humanitarian Actions (0–3 Months)

1. Address Acute Food, Water, and Medical Shortages

Iraq and the international aid community should address the main humanitarian issues identified in Mosul: the urgent shortage of food and water and the insufficiency of medical care. To address acute food insecurity, if the fighting in West Mosul becomes prolonged, Iraqi leaders and the UN should weigh options to address this (such as food drops, a temporary ceasefire, a managed evacuation, or other approaches), and the option chosen should receive the full support of the Coalition in implementation. To address the shortage of urgent health care, the United States and other donors should immediately increase funding and capacity for trauma stabilization points and field hospitals to be managed by the WHO. In addition, the United States and donors should fund sending additional doctors, nurses, surgeons, and specialists (particularly burn specialists and anesthesiologists) to the public hospitals in Erbil, Dohuk, and other nearby cities that are treating wounded civilians from Mosul, along with the provision of needed medical supplies. This recommendation also includes the opening of clinics and reconstruction of damaged hospitals in East Mosul and later in West Mosul as an urgent humanitarian need, not a long-term reconstruction objective.

2. Regularize Screening and Freedom of Movement for IDPs

The UN should negotiate with the KRG to ensure that basic norms are observed for IDPs in the camps. Among the measures to be agreed on are the following: The KRG should grant IDPs in camps freedom of movement and stop seizing identity cards. Iraqi Security Forces and peshmerga should complete the screening processes outside camps and ensure that international protection officers are present during screening, not only at the detention centers. The Iraqi government, KRG, and UN should take additional steps to quickly unify families separated into different camps. This includes funding NGOs in the camps to help IDPs navigate the family reunification processes; it also requires that the Iraqi government and KRG expedite permits to reunite families across provincial borders. The UN should provide mental health services to traumatized Iraqis in camps, make 24-hour physical health care available in the camps, and ensure protection officers are in all camps to monitor security and freedom of movement. To address water shortages that have emerged at the camps, the Coalition militaries should aid the Iraqi government and KRG in logistics to ensure that large quantities of drinking water are provided urgently and stocked for the future.

3. Promulgate and Begin to Implement a Safe IDP Return Policy

The Iraqi government and KRG should publish a concrete strategy with specific steps and metrics for fostering the safe return of all Iraqis who wish to go home. For those who do not wish to return home, the strategy should include options for local integration in their current locations or resettlement elsewhere when feasible. Different approaches will need to be taken based on the specific needs of individuals and communities. Specific steps should include addressing the concerns of all communities for protection against reprisals if they return, helping those who do not wish to return to their homes to resettle elsewhere in Iraq, assisting with investment to rebuild destroyed homes, aiding in the reunification of families, and establishing communication mechanisms for when areas are safe to return to. A specific government entity, determined by Prime Minister Haider al-Abadi, should be given this portfolio as its sole priority, with resources needed to execute it. Making a public commitment will send an important signal to the Sunni, Yazidi, Christian, Turkman, and other displaced populations of the Iraqi government's concern for their well-being. The government entity should also ensure that people displaced from areas now controlled by the KRG have the ability to return to their homes. Iraqi government and KRG officials said that there is no strategy for returns yet, but they signed a Memorandum of Understanding to do so. Donors should provide funding to the Iraqi government and KRG to develop this plan, with technical assistance from UN agencies like the UNHCR and IOM.

4. Expand the Scope and Pace of Explosive Hazard Mitigation

The United States and the international community should double funding and efforts for a tripartite demining program, as it is the most important physical factor in fostering the early return of Iraqis, their safety at home, access to public service infrastructure, and the resumption of their livelihood activities. The three prongs are as follows. First, Coalition members should increase aid for international demining (funding both humanitarian demining NGOs and private contractors such as Janus and Optima). This also includes fully funding the budget requests of UNMAS. Second, the institutional capability for a permanent Iraqi demining operation should be built. This includes scaling up the training of Iraqi employees of the NGOs and contractors. It also requires that the Coalition provide direct technical assistance to Iraq's demining institutions—the Directorate of Mine Action in Baghdad, the Iraqi Kurdish Mine Authority, the Iraqi security forces, and the peshmerga. Third, the Iraqi government should undertake a widespread public safety education program to inform Iraqis on how to avoid and manage mine hazards. This includes a public radio and television advertising campaign, education to children in Iraqi classrooms with a specially designed mine hazard curriculum, education of IDPs in camps in advance of their return to their homes, and a national demining website with information provided in Arabic, Kurdish, Turkman, and other relevant languages.

Expanded Stabilization (0–6 Months)

5. Ensure Adequate Hold Forces in Cleared Areas

Surveys and studies show that security is the fundamental criteria IDPs apply in deciding whether to return; many recovery activities vitally depend on it. Moreover, without security, ISIS may be able to retake liberated areas. Mosul's 1.2 million population requires a hold force of 60,000 troops to conduct near-term policing, establish checkpoints, and prevent looting and reprisals. These will be a mix of Iraqi army, Federal Police, Ninewa police, tribal, and minority forces. These forces must be adequately overseen by a duly constituted authority to ensure that their performance is sound and professional. Sufficient numbers of forces must be provided to ensure security in liberated areas and fend off ISIS attacks and efforts to mount a comeback. Given overall troop shortages and low levels of readiness, there is a significant risk that forces may be drawn off for onward military operations against ISIS in Tal Afar, Hawija, the Euphrates River Valley, or elsewhere in Iraq. The Iraqi government and the Coalition should ensure that, despite competing demands, adequate numbers of hold forces remain in place to keep the immediate peace and prevent new waves of violence from breaking out until fully trained police forces take their place.

6. Double Throughput of Police Training

Sufficient numbers of competent permanent police forces are needed to replace the temporary hold forces. This key security task should receive priority from the Iraqi government, the U.S. government, and other donors, reflected in increased funding and international trainers, as well as the adoption of a national plan. The production of the needed 16,700 police forces should be accelerated at least 100 percent by adding police trainers, without shortening or degrading the quality of the training. This would reduce the time needed to produce the force to 6 or 9 months, instead of the almost 18 months that would be required at the current pace. Additional training, vetting, and mentoring of those forces that have received brief instruction will also be needed. Arabic-speaking trainers would be desirable, and the Gulf States could play a productive role in providing these. Iraq's Ministry of Interior should be asked to demonstrate in concrete ways its professed commitment to professionalization and community policing models. Specifically, the revetting of forces to weed out sectarian actors should be prioritized.

7. Restore Public Services and Establish a Process to Resolve Property Disputes

The Iraqi government and Ninewa Province, with donor government assistance, should develop a prioritized public service, housing, and economic strategy for Mosul, with funding from multiple sources (e.g., the Iraqi government, World Bank loans, donor grants, or public-private partnerships with banks and companies). The UN, United States, and other donors should support the rapid accomplishment of a few key initiatives to deliver services and enable people to work and live in their homes. Although Mosul faces many needs, ramping up water, electricity, and educational access are vital. Water treatment plants and electricity facilities have been badly damaged, and restoration of their capacity to serve the city should be an urgent priority. Baghdad, Ninewa Province, and the UN should focus on increasing school capacity and implementing an education strategy (as half of the children in territory controlled by ISIS were out of school, were taught the ISIS curriculum, or were traumatized, and closed schools now prevent some IDP families from returning home). Quick action should be taken to start up civil service employment, with salaries reinstated from Baghdad for civil servants in Mosul who have cleared a vetting process. This should also include a plan for housing, with legal support for dealing with destroyed property records and minority housing sold by ISIS.

8. Improve Confidence in Ninewa Governance

Prime Minister Abadi should convene a Mosul transitional council under the authority of Baghdad to develop a plan for Ninewa governance postliberation and manage the immediate period postliberation. The transitional council should be a representative body and signal to Moslawis that they have a stake in their future. It should include officials from Baghdad and the KRG, as well as leaders of all communities (including Sunnis, Shia, Christians, Yazidis, and Turkman), tribal leaders, leading businesspeople, religious leaders, and local politicians. It should develop a vision for Ninewa, rebuilding priorities, economic priorities, and presentation of existing plans. Prime Minister Abadi, the U.S. government, the UN, and other donor governments should provide direct diplomatic, financial, and logistical support to this body in their local reconciliation work, negotiations, and regional publicity campaigns.

Governance and Political Reconciliation (0–12 Months)

9. Implement Decentralization Law

The U.S. government should renew its funding to support implementation of the decentralization law and advocate prioritization of this measure by the Baghdad government. The delivery of services at the local level is a critical means to restore and increase public confidence in government. Decentralization is a long-term project, given the history of highly centralized Baathist government. USAID should renew its Governance Strengthening Project to continue supporting the implementation of Iraq's decentralization law and training of local government officials to assume the functions devolved from the central government. This would enable continued and accelerated devolution of functions of eight ministries, as authorized in current law. While there is a new USAID program to increase competence and oversight of fiscal management (apart from decentralization), implementation of the decentralization law will likely languish or stall entirely without continued USAID technical support. The law envisions devolution of authorities for another five ministries, including the finance ministry. The renewed USAID programs should include particular emphasis on and technical assistance to the provinces most affected by ISIS: Ninewa, Anbar, Salah al-Din, Diyala, and Kirkuk.

10. Improve Public Finance and Public Management

The U.S. government should adopt World Bank performance standards and tie its assistance under the Strategic Framework Agreement to agreed-on transparency and accountability measures. To encourage Iraqi government performance and accountability, the United States should throw its weight behind the newly established UNDP Economic Reform Fund, supported by the World Bank, to help implement economic reforms and anticorruption measures at the national level.[1] To build long-term Iraqi competence during the stabilization process and beyond, the United States

---

[1] Searching 4 Dinar, "The Government Signed a Project Document in Baghdad to Establish 'Economic Reform Fund,'" *Searching 4 Dinar*, January 29, 2017. As of March 27, 2017: https://search4dinar.wordpress.com/2017/01/29/the-government-signed-a-project-document-in-baghdad-to-establish-economic-reform-fund/.

should back the creation of a secretariat or project management unit within the Iraq Ministry of Planning, which can serve as a means for coordinating bilateral assistance to the Iraqi government; the unit would in turn coordinate with the KRG Ministry of Planning and Joint Coordination Centre. This is an approach that has been implemented elsewhere to enable accountable bilateral assistance.[2]

11. Expand and Coordinate Local Reconciliation Programs

Donors such as the United States, Germany, the United Kingdom, and the EU should increase funding to grassroots reconciliation efforts through the U.S. Institute of Peace, UNDP, IOM, and Iraqi NGOs. A coordinating body should prioritize and deconflict efforts to ensure areas of critical needs are served. These activities should also be coordinated with the new UNDP program that focuses on three separate but mutually supporting initiatives: a media campaign highlighting the benefits of reconciliation; facilitation of civil society groups to convene local community discussions nationwide; and a memory project that will archive accounts of abuses and atrocities as a basis for future transitional justice agreements. Other urgent needs highlighted by UN and other experts are negotiations among particular aggrieved local communities and psychological counseling programs as part of this bottom-up effort.

12. Jump-Start National Reconciliation with a Road Map and a Group of Friends

These grassroots efforts should be simultaneously paired with a carefully constructed national effort supported by the UN. The U.S. government should take the lead in forming a multicountry Group of Friends to provide high-visibility support to the Iraqi government and the UN Assistance Mission for Iraq to create a national settlement road map that will provide basic security, revenues, and resettlement aid to Sunni areas. A road map might be outlined in draft form before the next Iraqi national elections, but the implementation of key steps, such as revised justice and accountability laws, further devolution of authorities to provinces, possible provincial security forces, and resolution of Kirkuk's status, would likely have to await formation of a new government. Sustained talks supported by the UN should commence on the basis of the road map. To incentivize this process, multiyear funding for the U.S.-Iraqi Strategic Framework Agreement implementation plan could be tied to agreement on a road map and the commencement of talks.

Reconciliation depends in part on accountability. There must be accountability for individuals who committed atrocities against civilians and took up arms against their government—but without collective punishment of groups for the behavior of individuals. There should be a rapid mechanism established for due process for criminals who committed crimes. At the same time, issuing an amnesty and releasing imprisoned Sunnis who are not charged with any crime will provide an immediate surge in Sunni

---

2 Culbertson et al., 2016.

Iraqis' confidence at a critical juncture. Although some Shia might criticize this latter action, Prime Minister Abadi possesses the executive authority to issue an amnesty, in conjunction with the establishment of accountability mechanisms, and he would gain major credibility with Sunnis, who fear reprisals and recriminations from those who blame all Sunnis for the ISIS depredations.

Financial Burden Sharing

13. Accelerate Funding

The United States should urge the UN and the Iraqi government to call for all pledged funding to be delivered in the current calendar year to enable accelerated stabilization. In addition, realistic estimates of future funding needs should be developed. Significant funds are required for the humanitarian response, stabilization, and eventual reconstruction of liberated areas of Iraq. While initial expectations were that Iraq, as an oil state, would fund much of the stabilization and all of the reconstruction, the low price of oil and Iraq's financial crisis have impeded that. Iraq's resources will eventually allow it to assume larger portions of the rebuilding bill, but its current financial crisis makes it dependent on international funding for stabilization.[3] Other financing mechanisms should be explored as well, such as additional World Bank, Islamic Development Bank, or other loans with concessional financing, or public-private partnerships to finance infrastructure rebuilding. The United States should renew efforts to solicit Gulf donors (particularly Saudi Arabia, the United Arab Emirates, Kuwait, and Qatar), which have been reluctant to fund stabilization and recovery efforts in Iraq because they have suspicions about Iranian influence, concerns over Prime Minister Abadi's capabilities in reconciliation, and concerns about the corruption of the Iraqi government.[4] However, Saudi Arabia provided $500 million early in the conflict, the United Arab Emirates provided $50 million, and Kuwait recently provided emergency funding for Mosul in addition to delaying reparations payments owed by Iraq for the 1991 Gulf War. The World Bank should provide technical assistance to the Iraqi government to develop an Iraqi rebuilding investment prospectus that describes specific rebuilding projects that donors, including the Gulf countries, should be asked to fund: particularly, roads, bridges, electrical stations, hospitals, schools, and university buildings.

---

[3] Iraq had two economic shocks: the fall of the price of oil, and war with ISIS. Of Iraq's revenues, 90 percent are from oil, and the government is faced with a financing gap of $18 billion. The International Monetary Fund's $5.34 billion loan in 2016 and $1.2 billion in 2015 include funding for IDPs and social services for the vulnerable. Despite disruption in production and trade routes that hit the nonoil economy, the oil sector grew by 13 percent in 2015 and 20 percent in 2016.

[4] Hardin Lang and Muath Al Wari, "After Liberation: Assessing Stabilization Efforts in Areas of Iraq Cleared of the Islamic State," Center for American Progress, July 26, 2016. As of March 27, 2017: https://www.americanprogress.org/issues/security/reports/2016/07/26/141814/after-liberation/.

14. Increase Transparency and Accountability of Funding

The creation of a comprehensive online site and the institution of procedures to track all donations from pledging through commitment to implementation would greatly increase donor confidence that their funds are being used for the intended purposes. At present, a central picture of donor funding for humanitarian assistance and stabilization in Iraq is lacking. Increased efficiencies can also be sought to ensure that the assistance provides maximum benefit. For example, further measures can be instituted to report and, as possible, reduce subcontracting costs. Both UN and Iraqi officials noted the inefficiency of UN funding mechanisms, caused by high overhead charges and chains of subcontracting—for example, from one UN agency subcontracting to another, which subcontracts to an implementing NGO or private company, which subcontracts to another implementing NGO or private company. This inefficient management of resources in UN-managed responses has been documented in other studies of the financial management of displacement crises. UNOCHA should create a continuous online mechanism that transparently tracks donor funding for humanitarian activity and the stabilization of Iraq, including funding commitments, how and where donor funding is spent, which entities receive this funding, criteria for the selection of projects and programs, and specific accounting of overheads and pass-through contracting. The government of Iraq would also need to assist in providing or overseeing validated reporting and on-site verification of project work.

Looking Ahead

Iraq is not hopeless. It is a country with a wealth of human capacity, natural resources, and world heritage. Iraqis have demonstrated great resolve and resourcefulness in combatting ISIS and coordinating with the Coalition and the international aid community. Iraqi communities have shown their generosity of spirit by hosting other Iraqis displaced by fighting and persecution. After the recent decades of instability, many Iraqis are willing to take steps to move their country onward. Yet, Iraqis cannot achieve this alone—stability in Iraq, and resulting stability elsewhere in the Middle East, depends on active leadership and financial and technical support from the United States, other Coalition members, the neighboring Gulf States, and the United Nations system. In this report, we have aimed to provide a set of targeted steps that can create a foundation for and momentum toward these goals. But without fast progress in these fundamental areas, Iraq risks devolving once again into instability, with resulting implications for the security of Iraq's neighbors and allies.

Selected Bibliography

Amnesty International, *Punished for Daesh's Crimes: Displaced Iraqis Abused by Militias and Government Forces*, New York, October 18, 2016.

Arango, Tim, and Helene Cooper, "U.S. Investigating Mosul Strikes Said to Have Killed up to 200 Civilians," *New York Times*, March 29, 2017.

Arango, Tim, and Rick Gladstone, "Retaking Mosul from ISIS May Pale to What Comes Next," *New York Times*, October 18, 2016. As of March 16, 2017:
https://www.nytimes.com/2016/10/19/world/middleeast/mosul-iraq-isis.html

Arraf, Jane, "How Ramadi Was Won," *Newsweek*, February 22, 2016.

Browne, Gareth, "Meet the U.S. Volunteers Treating Patients at a Front Line Clinic in Mosul," *Middle East Eye*, December 18, 2016. As of March 24, 2017:
http://www.middleeasteye.net/in-depth/features/meet-volunteers-front-line-clinic-mosul-1822411855

Chairman of the Joint Chiefs of Staff, "Joint Publication 3-07: Stability," United States Department of Defense, August 3, 2016. As of March 27, 2017:
http://www.dtic.mil/doctrine/new_pubs/jp3_07.pdf

Chulov, Martin, "Iraqi Forces Seize Mosul Airport from Isis as Syrian Rebels Take Al-Bab," *Guardian*, February 24, 2017. As of March 24, 2017:
https://www.theguardian.com/world/2017/feb/23/iraqi-forces-storm-mosul-airport-seize-isis

Culbertson, Shelly, Olga Oliker, Ben Baruch, and Ilana Blum. *Rethinking Coordination of Services to Refugees in Urban Areas: Managing the Crisis in Jordan and Lebanon*, RAND, 2016. As of June 12, 2017:
https://www.rand.org/pubs/research_reports/RR1485.html

DeLuce, Dan, and Henry Johnson, "Who Will Rule Mosul?," *Foreign Policy*, April 29, 2016. As of March 27, 2017:
http://foreignpolicy.com/2016/04/29/iraq-isis-sunni-shiite-kurds-fight-mosul/

Dolmari, Mewan, "Nineveh to Be Divided into Eight Provinces: Former Governor," *Kurdistan24*, September 8, 2016. As of March 19, 2017:
http://www.kurdistan24.net/en/news/2e0926ae-87ad-4a8b-a39e-60b9bcc6baec/Nineveh-to-be-divided-into-eight-provinces—Former-Governor

Erbil Refugee Council, United Nations High Commission for Refugees (UNHCR), Erbil Statistics Directorate, Joint Crisis Coordination Centre, International Organization for Migration (IOM), United Nations Population Fund, United Nations Human Settlements Programme (UN-Habitat), and United Nations Office for the Coordination of Humanitarian Affairs (UNOCHA), *Displacement as Challenge and Opportunity, Urban Profile of Refugees, Internally Displaced Persons and Host Community: Erbil Governorate, Kurdistan Region of Iraq*, May 2016. As of March 28, 2017:
http://reliefweb.int/sites/reliefweb.int/files/resources/ErbilUrbanProfilingApril2016English.pdf

Gordon, Michael R., "U.S. Forces Play Crucial Role Against ISIS in Mosul," *New York Times*, February 26, 2017a. As of March 24, 2017:
https://www.nytimes.com/2017/02/26/world/middleeast/mosul-iraq-american-military-role-islamic-state.html

———, "U.S. 'Probably Had a Role' in Mosul Deaths, Commander Says," *New York Times*, March 28, 2017b.

Inter-Agency Information and Analysis Unit and United Nations Office for the Coordination of Humanitarian Affairs (OCHA), *Governorate Profile for Ninewa*, December 2010.

Internal Displacement Monitoring Centre, "Iraq: IDPs Caught Between a Rock and a Hard Place as Displacement Crisis Deepens," June 30, 2015. As of March 27, 2017:
http://www.internal-displacement.org/middle-east-and-north-africa/iraq/2015/iraq-idps-caught-between-a-rock-and-a-hard-place-as-displacement-crisis-deepens

International Organization for Migration (IOM): Iraq Mission, "Displacement Tracking Matrix | DTM," UN Migration Agency, March 16, 2017a. Time series October 2016–April 1, 2017. As of March 27, 2017:
http://iraqdtm.iom.int/IDPsML.aspx

———, "Displacement Tracking Matrix: Factsheet #36—Mosul Operations from 17 October to 06 July," 2017. As of July 7, 2017:
http://iraqdtm.iom.int/Downloads/DTM%20Emergency%20Tracking/Mosul%20Crisis/1-Mosul%20Operations%20Factsheets/DTM%20ET%20Mosul%20Operations%20Factsheet%20%2336.pdf

———, "Displacement Tracking Matrix: IDP Locations & Population, January 2014–May 26, 2016," 2016a. As of March 27, 2017:
http://reliefweb.int/sites/reliefweb.int/files/resources/Round46_Map_Location_Population_2016_May_26_IOM_DTM.pdf

———, "Iraq Mission: Displacement Tracking Matrix | DTM," UN Migration Agency, March 23, 2017b. As of March 27, 2017:
http://iraqdtm.iom.int/EmergencyTracking.aspx

———, "Ninewa Governorate Profile, May 2015," 2015. As of March 27, 2017:
http://iomiraq.net/reports/ninewa-governorate-profile-may-2015

———, "Returnee Location Assessment Report," *ReliefWeb*, October 2016b. As of March 27, 2017:
http://reliefweb.int/sites/reliefweb.int/files/resources/IOM%20DTM%20Returnee%20Location%20Assessment%20Report_October_2016.pdf

Joint Publication 1-02, *Department of Defense Dictionary of Military and Associated Terms*, as amended through March 15, 2012, Washington, D.C.: Joint Chiefs of Staff, 2012.

Jones, Rupert, "News Transcript: Department of Defense Press Briefing by Maj. Gen. Jones via Teleconference from Baghdad, Iraq," U.S. Department of Defense, February 15, 2017. As of March 27, 2017:
https://www.defense.gov/News/Transcripts/Transcript-View/Article/1084947/department-of-defense-press-briefing-by-maj-gen-jones-via-teleconference-from-b?source=GovDelivery

Kalin, Stephen, "Iraqi Military Freezes Civilians' Return to Ramadi over Mine Deaths," Reuters, April 24, 2016. As of March 24, 2017:
http://www.reuters.com/article/us-mideast-crisis-iraq-ramadi-idUSKCN0XL0OL

Kossov, Igor, "Mosul's Growing Humanitarian Crisis as Bad as Feared," *USA Today*, March 15, 2017. As of March 24, 2017:
http://www.usatoday.com/story/news/world/2017/03/15/mosul-refugees-iraq-camps/99137150/

Kurdistan Region of Iraq Erbil Governorate, *Displacement as Challenge and Opportunity, Erbil Profile*, April 2016.

Lang, Hardin, and Muath Al Wari, "After Liberation: Assessing Stabilization Efforts in Areas of Iraq Cleared of the Islamic State," Center for American Progress, July 26, 2016. As of March 27, 2017: https://www.americanprogress.org/issues/security/reports/2016/07/26/141814/after-liberation/

Mamouri, Ali, "Is It Time for a National Settlement in Iraq?," *Al-Monitor*, November 9, 2016. As of March 27, 2017:
http://www.al-monitor.com/pulse/en/originals/2016/11/national-reconciliation-iraq-shiite-kurd-sunni.html

McCoy, Terrence, "ISIS Just Stole $425 Million, Iraqi Governor Says, and Became the 'World's Richest Terrorist Group,'" *Washington Post*, June 12, 2014.

"Mosul Battle: Iraq Forces 'Retake' University from IS," *BBC News*, January 14, 2017. As of March 24, 2017:
http://www.bbc.com/news/world-middle-east-38623671

"Mosul Battle: Triple Car Bomb Attack Kills 23 at Market," *BBC News*, December 22, 2016. As of March 28, 2017:
http://www.bbc.com/news/world-middle-east-38406631

Neurink, Judit, "Tikrit University Brings Life Back to Saddam's Hometown," *Rudaw*, June 6, 2016. As of May 1, 2017:
http://www.rudaw.net/english/middleeast/iraq/060620161

Organisation for Economic Cooperation and Development, "Humanitarian Assistance," 2016. As of March 27, 2017:
http://www.oecd.org/dac/stats/humanitarian-assistance.htm

Osgood, Patrick, Rawaz Tahir, and *Iraq Oil Report* staff, "IS Use of Human Shields Complicated Mosul Offensive," Iraq Oil Report, March 31, 2017. As of March 31, 2017:
http://www.iraqoilreport.com/news/use-human-shields-complicates-mosul-offensive-21900/

O'Toole, Megan, "How Will Mosul Rise from the Ashes of Battle?," *Al Jazeera*, November 12, 2016. As of March 27, 2017:
http://www.aljazeera.com/indepth/features/2016/11/mosul-rise-ashes-battle-161112100900149.html.

Partland, Lily, and Simon Edmunds, *Over a Million Children Living Under ISIS in Iraq Have Missed Out on Education: Save the Children*, Save the Children, November 6, 2016.

"Press Briefing by Press Secretary Josh Earnest and Special Envoy for the Global Coalition to Counter ISIL, Brett McGurk," White House: Office of the Press Secretary, December 13, 2016. As of March 24, 2017:
https://obamawhitehouse.archives.gov/the-press-office/2016/12/13/press-briefing-press-secretary-josh-earnest-and-special-envoy-global

"Press Conference by SPE [Special Presidential Envoy] Mcgurk in Baghdad, Iraq," U.S. Department of State, October 25, 2016. As of March 28, 2017:
https://2009-2017.state.gov/s/seci/263568.htm

Quinlivan, James T., "Burden of Victory: The Painful Arithmetic of Stability Operations," *RAND Review*, Vol. 27, No. 2, Summer 2003, p. 200.

———, "Force Requirements in Stability Operations," *Parameters*, Vol. 25, No. 4, 1995, pp. 59–60.

Rasheed, Ahmed, "Islamic State Readies for Close Combat in Alleyways of West Mosul," Reuters, February 17, 2017. As of March 27, 2017:
http://www.reuters.com/article/us-mideast-crisis-iraq-mosul-idUSKBN15W1GY

REACH, *Assessment of Eight Hard-to-Reach Areas in Iraq, 2015–2016*, June 2016. As of March 27, 2017:
https://www.sheltercluster.org/sites/default/files/docs/reach_irq_report_assessment_of_eight_hard-to-reach_areas_in_iraq_july_2016.pdf

Reuters, "Mosul's East Begins to Bustle but Healing a Long Way Off," *New York Times*, March 24, 2017. As of March 28, 2017:
https://www.nytimes.com/reuters/2017/03/24/world/middleeast/24reuters-mideast-crisis-iraq-mosul-residents.html?_r=0

Robinson, Linda, Todd Helmus, Raphael Cohen, Ali Nader, Andrew Radin, Madeline Magnuson, and Katya Migacheva, *Assessment of the Politico-Military Campaign to Counter ISIL and Options for Adaptation*, Santa Monica, Calif.: RAND Corporation, 2016.

———, *Modern Political Warfare: Current Practices and Possible Responses*, Santa Monica, Calif.: RAND Corporation, forthcoming.

Rudaw, "Abadi Promises Mosul Leaders Decentralized Governance After Liberation," July 26, 2016. As of April 10, 2017:
http://rudaw.net/english/middleeast/iraq/260720161

Sattar, Omar, "How Iraq's PMU Law Is Disrupting National Unity Efforts," *Al Monitor*, December 14, 2016. As of March 27, 2017:
http://www.al-monitor.com/pulse/originals/2016/12/national-settlement-pmu-law-iraq.html#

Searching 4 Dinar, "The Government Signed a Project Document in Baghdad to Establish 'Economic Reform Fund,'" *Searching 4 Dinar*, January 29, 2017. As of March 27, 2017:
https://search4dinar.wordpress.com/2017/01/29/the-government-signed-a-project-document-in-baghdad-to-establish-economic-reform-fund/

Sphere Project, "The Sphere Handbook." As of March 24, 2017:
http://www.spherehandbook.org/

Stabilisation Unit, "The UK Government's Approach to Stabilisation," UK Foreign and Commonwealth Office, UK Ministry of Defence, and UK Department for International Development, May 2014. As of March 27, 2017:
http://www.sclr.stabilisationunit.gov.uk/attachments/article/520/TheUKApproachtoStabilisationMay2014.pdf

"UN Agency Cuts Food Aid to 1.4 Million Displaced Iraqis," *Al Jazeera*, January 28, 2017. As of March 28, 2017:
http://www.aljazeera.com/news/2017/01/food-aid-displaced-iraqis-170128051248193.html

UN Assistance Mission for Iraq, "Briefing to the Security Council by Srsg for Iraq Ján Kubiš; New York, 9 November 2016 [En/Ar]," *ReliefWeb*, November 9, 2016. As of March 24, 2017:
http://reliefweb.int/report/iraq/briefing-security-council-srsg-iraq-j-n-kubi-new-york-9-november-2016-enar

United Nations Children's Fund (UNICEF), "Humanitarians Fear for the 750,000 Civilians in Western Mosul," January 24, 2017a. As of March 24, 2017:
https://www.unicef.org/media/media_94438.html

———, "Reaching Children in Iraq," February 10, 2017b. As of March 24, 2017:
https://www.unicef.org/infobycountry/iraq_74784.html

United Nations Development Programme (UNDP) in Iraq, "About Iraq," 2017. As of March 24, 2017:
http://www.iq.undp.org/content/iraq/en/home/countryinfo.html

———, *Funding Facility for Immediate Stabilization: Quarterly Progress Report, Q3—Year 2016*, 2016a.

———, "Tikrit: A Stabilization Success Following Liberation from ISIL," July 20, 2016b. As of March 27, 2017:
http://www.iq.undp.org/content/iraq/en/home/ourwork/Stabilization/our-stories/stabilization-in-tikrit.html

United Nations High Commission for Refugees (UNHCR): The UN Refugee Agency, *UNHCR Policy on Refugee Protection and Solutions in Urban Areas,* September 2009. As of March 28, 2017:
http://www.unhcr.org/4ab356ab6.pdf

United Nations Humanitarian Country Team, "2016 Humanitarian Response Plan: Iraq," United Nations Office for the Coordination of Humanitarian Affairs, December 2015. As of March 27, 2017:
http://reliefweb.int/sites/reliefweb.int/files/resources/final_iraq_2016_hrp.pdf

United Nations Human Settlements Programme (UN-Habitat), *City Profile of Mosul, Iraq: Multi-Sectoral Assessment of a City under Siege,* October 2016. As of June 14, 2017:
https://unhabitat.org/city-profile-of-mosul-iraq-a-city-under-siege/

———, *Mosul Data & Mapping Portal: Physical Damage Assessment,* January 31, 2017a.

———, *Rapid Situation Assessment: Living Conditions on the Right Bank of Mosul,* February 2, 2017b.

United Nations Iraq, "UN Casualties Figures for Iraq for the Month of December 2016," January 3, 2017a. As of March 27, 2017:
http://www.uniraq.org/index.php?option=com_k2&view=item&id=6611:un-casualties-figures-for-iraq-for-the-month-of-december-2016&Itemid=633&lang=en

———, "UN Casualties Figures for Iraq for the Month of January 2017," February 2, 2017b. As of March 27, 2017:
http://www.uniraq.org/index.php?option=com_k2&view=item&id=6725:un-casualties-figures-for-iraq-for-the-month-of-january-2017&Itemid=633&lang=en

———, "UN Casualty Figures for Iraq for the Month of November 2016," December 2, 2016c. As of March 27, 2017:
http://www.uniraq.org/index.php?option=com_k2&view=item&id=6455:un-casualty-figures-for-iraq-for-the-month-of-november-2016&Itemid=633&lang=en

———, "UN Casualty Figures for Iraq for the Month of October 2016," November 1, 2016a. As of March 27, 2017:
http://www.uniraq.org/index.php?option=com_k2&view=item&id=6267:un-casualty-figures-for-iraq-for-the-month-of-october-2016&Itemid=633&lang=en

———, "Unicef: Iraq Crisis Flash Update #1: Mosul Response 17–31 October 2016," November 2, 2016b. As of March 24, 2017:
http://uniraq.org/index.php?option=com_k2&view=item&id=6278:unicef-iraq-crisis-flash-update-1-mosul-response-17-31-october-2016&Itemid=626&lang=en

United Nations Office for the Coordination of Humanitarian Affairs (UNOCHA), *Iraq Humanitarian Response Plan,* June 2015. As of March 24, 2017:
http://reliefweb.int/sites/reliefweb.int/files/resources/2015-Iraq-Humanitarian-Response-Plan%20%281%29.pdf

———, "Iraq: Mosul Humanitarian Response Situation Report #7, (7–13 November 2016) [En/Ar/Ku]," *ReliefWeb,* November 14, 2016b. As of March 24, 2017:
http://reliefweb.int/report/iraq/iraq-mosul-humanitarian-response-situation-report-7-7-13-november-2016-enarku

———, *Mosul Flash Appeal,* July 20, 2016a. As of March 24, 2017:
https://docs.unocha.org/sites/dms/Iraq/mosul_flash_appeal_final_web%20(1).pdf

UN News Centre, "Humanitarian Crisis in Mosul Could Outlive Iraqi Military Operations, Senior UN Official Warns," United Nations, 2017. As of March 27, 2017:
http://www.un.org/apps/news/story.asp?NewsID=55948#.WJtkEBiZMmJ

UN Refugee Agency, "UNHCR Mosul Weekly Protection Update," United Nations, March 11–17, 2017. Time series reports October 2016–April 2017. As of March 27, 2017:
http://reliefweb.int/sites/reliefweb.int/files/resources/UNHCR%20Mosul%20Weekly%20Protection%20Update%2011-17%20Mar.pdf

United States Agency for International Development (USAID) Iraq and Governance Strengthening Project—Taqadum, *Special Report on Ninewa: Post-Conflict Actions Taken in Liberated Areas*, September 2016.

"Update on Campaign Against ISIL: Special Briefing by Brett Mcgurk, Special Presidential Envoy for the Global Coalition to Counter ISIL," U.S. Department of State, October 6, 2016. As of March 28, 2017:
https://2009-2017.state.gov/r/pa/prs/ps/2016/10/262934.htm

World Bank, *Republic of Iraq: Decentralization and Subnational Service Delivery in Iraq: Status and Way Forward*, March 2016. As of March 27, 2017:
http://documents.worldbank.org/curated/en/583111468043159983/pdf/Iraq-Decentralization-JIT-Assessment-Report-March-2016-FINAL.pdf